The Memoirs of a True Believer in Christ

with views, opinions, and facts

B.L. Scott

BK Royston Publishing
P. O. Box 4321
Jeffersonville, IN 47131
502-802-5385
http://www.bkroystonpublishing.com
bkroystonpublishing@gmail.com

© Copyright – 2020

All Rights Reserved. No part of this book may be reproduced, stored in a retrieval system, or transmitted by any means without the written permission of the author.

Cover Design: Elite Book Covers

ISBN: 978-1-951941-08-6

English Standard Version **(ESV)** The Holy Bible, English Standard Version. ESV® Text Edition: 2016. Copyright © 2001 by Crossway Bibles, a publishing ministry of Good News Publishers.

King James Version (KJV) - Public Domain

Printed in the United States of America

"The king declared to Daniel, whose name was Belteshazzar, "Are you able to make known to me the dream that I have seen and its interpretation?" Daniel answered the king and said, "No wise men, enchanters, magicians, or astrologers can show to the king the mystery that the king has asked, but there is a God in heaven who reveals mysteries, and he has made known to King Nebuchadnezzar what will be in the latter days. Your dream and the visions of your head as you lay in bed are these: To you, O king, as you lay in bed came thoughts of what would be after this, and he who reveals mysteries made known to you what is to be. To you, O king, as you lay in bed came thoughts of what would be after this, and he who reveals mysteries made known to you what is to be. But as for me, this mystery has been revealed to me, not because of any wisdom that I have more than all the living, but in order that the interpretation may be made known to the king, and that you may know the thoughts of your mind."

Daniel 2:26-30 (ESV)

Dedication

**I'd like to dedicate this series of books to my Beautiful,
Loving Wife
and my Amazing
Daughter**

Mother and Child

The Love between mother and child,
molds the will of the meek and mild...
Shows of affection by one so great,
always ever present, never early, never late...
To build off this feeling is more than a fact,
This Love defines more than just a mere act...
Of intellect measures and forms of concentration,
Like the summer morning due from a rose petals condensation..
With something so complex but simple to its nature,
Almost like a fairy tale ending, wise to its legislature...
Coming to fruition but never settling for an end,
This Love between mother and child is from God, that's where it will begin.....

Table of Contents

Dedication		iv
Mother and Child		v
Introduction		viii
Preface		xiii
Warrior's Creed		xviii
Chapter One	Revelations	1
Clean Heart		44
Chapter Two	Heaven	45
For His Glory		62
Chapter Three	Hell	65
Souls at Night		92

Job 8:7 (ESV)

"And though your beginning was small, your latter days will be very great."

Proverbs 8:23 (ESV)

"Ages ago I was set up, at the first, before the beginning of the earth."

Ecclesiastes 3:11 (ESV)

"He has made everything beautiful in its time. Also, he has put eternity into man's heart, yet so that he cannot find out what God has done from the beginning to the end."

1 John 2:12 – 14 (ESV)

"I am writing to you, little children, because your sins are forgiven for his name's sake. I am writing to you, fathers, because you know him who is from the beginning. I am writing to you, young men, because you have overcome the evil one. I write to you, children, because you know the Father. I write to you, fathers, because you know him who is from the beginning. I write to you, young men, because you are strong, and the word of God abides in you, and you have overcome the evil one."

Introduction

Matthew 6:31-33 (ESV)

"Therefore, do not be anxious, saying, 'What shall we eat?' or 'What shall we drink?' or 'What shall we wear?' For the Gentiles seek after all these things, and your heavenly Father knows that you need them all. But seek first the kingdom of God and his righteousness, and all these things will be added to you."

Hello,

What I'm about to share with you is exactly what has happened to me with my visions and dreams given to me from God our Father. To this day, I still have prophetic dreams but not the visons. Some of the topics that I will share with you are controversial in some eyes. Some of the topics that I will discuss in these books will make some angered while many others will agree. Some will mock these writings as if I either made all of it up, or they will act as though I don't know what I am talking about. Most of the ones that will mock this writing will be other Christians. One thing is for certain... God our father sees us without fault. God our father sees us as the same as Jesus Christ, so don't grieve Him and lose your reward. Be saved and lean towards the Wisdom of God, not yourself!

We Do not have enough time left; our time is short!

When He touched down, that very moment changed forever and as He touched me. I was changed forever...
As He held this clay in His mighty hands, He formed it with love a thousand times over. Deep within His chest came an exhale of air which came from His lungs into this frail creation, and now I have a purpose...
God had the breath of life come forth, and in that unforgettable moment, I witnessed life being born in the Kingdom of God that could not be measured by any possible reason...
Now realizing that I'm in the spirit realm which resides in another dimension, I turned my head to find something so immeasurable in size and wealth...
I fell to my knees and knew that I was in the throne room which had an overwhelming presence, but I couldn't figure out why I was crying...
Maybe it was because I saw a chamber with my name on it, and right away I knew that it held records of my entire life in it....
Or maybe it's because of the awesome stone that I'm holding that has my name written on it....

Jeremiah 46: 9 & 10 (ESV)

"Advance, O horses, and rage, O chariots! Let the warriors go out: men of Cush and Put who handle the shield, men of Lud, skilled in handling the bow. That day is the day of the Lord GOD of hosts, a day of vengeance, to avenge himself on his foes. The sword shall devour and be sated and drink its fill of their blood. For the Lord GOD of hosts holds a sacrifice in the north country by the river Euphrates."

Joel 2: 7 – 11 (ESV)

"Like warriors they charge; like soldiers they scale the wall. They march each on his way; they do not swerve from their paths. They do not jostle one another; each marches in his path; they burst through the weapons and are not halted.

They leap upon the city, they run upon the walls, they climb up into the houses, they enter through the windows like a thief. The earthquakes before them; the heavens tremble. Sun and the moon are darkened, and the stars withdraw their shining. The LORD utters his voice before his army, for his camp is exceedingly great; he who executes his word is powerful. For the day of the LORD is great and very awesome; who can endure it?"

Preface

Once more, some people will like and respect this writing and some will dismiss this writing, but it's so important to let God have His way in your life! I hope you truly read, understand and come to like this; I didn't just write for my own health. To the ones that like to disprove anything that may lift someone up or shine the light of Jesus to the World, this is for you... If you're trying to debunk or deface these writings, be sure to understand that I will not debate anything that has to do with these writings or discuss the reason or why I wrote these words. If you want to deface, discredit or debunk this book or its content, then I suggest that you read The Word of God for yourself!

I will not ever talk about why I wrote these books or anything like its content, if it means that God our Father isn't behind your questioning and reasoning.

"Don't let your heart be hardened, don't let your love grow cold...." ~Petra

Acts 17:24-32 (ESV)

"The God who made the world and everything in it, being Lord of heaven and earth, does not live in temples made by man, nor is he served by human hands, as though he needed anything, since he himself gives to all mankind life and breath and everything.

And he made from one man every nation of mankind to live on all the face of the earth, having determined allotted periods and the boundaries of their dwelling place, that they should seek God, in the hope that they might feel their way toward him and find him. Yet he is actually not far from each one of us, for "'In him we live and move and have our being'; as even some of your own poets have said, "'For we are indeed his offspring.'

Being then God's offspring, we ought not to think that the divine being is like gold or silver or stone, an image formed by the art and imagination of man.

The times of ignorance God overlooked, but now he commands all people everywhere to repent, because he has fixed a day on which He will judge the world in righteousness by a man whom he has appointed; and of this he has given assurance to all by raising him from the dead." Now when they heard of the resurrection of the dead, some mocked. But others said, "We will hear you again about this."

Did you know that God is raising up Champions of His own; Warriors in Christ, in these modern times to display, teach, preach and perform miracles in the power of the name of Jesus? With the power of God, the Father, the Blood of the Lamb and the presence of the Holy Spirit, champions are being raised. Champions like Moses, Jacob, Joseph, Samson, David, Ester and the list goes on.

Only real champions can realize that God is about to call them to do something they are totally incapable of doing. Champions must be prepared for their own actions; they must be Purged for God to use them to their fullest potential. God our Father had to purge these individuals so they could be his champions. For instance, Jacob wrestled with an Angel, Moses confronted a Pharaoh and Joseph became a slave only later to become a Ruler!

Everyone loves a champion. Champions gain people's hearts. They also have this incredible ability to intertwine themselves in and around people.

Psalms 105:18&19 (ESV)
"His feet were hurt with fetters; his neck was put in a collar of iron; until what he had said came to pass, the word of the LORD tested him."

Don't go off halfcocked with so much zeal that you forget wisdom. You might end up incarcerated, and then you'll be waiting on God to get you out only to find that He was purging you into a Warring Champion!

What are some signs of a Rising Warrior?

They grow to have a knowledge that they were born for such a time as this in which having such a belief. They are believing that God will prepare them for

something greater. Although, they may not understand at first, their trust is that God our Father is ironclad. These rising warriors will not allow life's circumstances to dictate or define their future. They also learn how to be successful in serving another person's vision until their vision comes to fruition. They know that when God is ready, His Word will come to pass. They have learned to wait on the Lord and to celebrate the presence of the Lord.

- John Paul Jackson-

We must come to a place where our sufficiency is in God and not in ourselves, where our confidence is not in ourselves but in God, and we must also recognize the importance of reaching the realization of righteousness meaning more to us then grace.

If you allow Him too, God will remove and expose your personal agendas and anger for your benefit. How else would you grow if you wouldn't allow God to do what He needs to do inside of you?

Anything that God can do for you will also give Him the glory as you get the victory. So, He will receive the glory when the Word comes to pass, but you must choose because God gave you the Choice.

When God made us, Humanity, Man and Woman, it was perfect in His eyes because we are His Creation and everything about us is designed to influence good. We have to abide constantly in God and know His ways as His creation. He is our Father and we are His children, and there must be no doubt in our hearts that God will back us up when we need Him. We are supposed to be His Warriors.

The world needs to see God in our lives, and the world needs to see Jesus through us. In one of his conferences, John Paul Jackson said this, "Close proximity to God is what allows him to radiate through us." You need to be in a place where you are the light shining in a dark area. A place where that light would be Jesus Christ because you are living your life right, and you are following hard after a Christ like heart just like David did.

We need to be a light in a dark world. If we are amongst sinners and non-believers and they see us as one of their own, then we have failed God. We Have Failed God!

Be of the World, and not in it. Don't be a part of the World, or your soul could be at risk for ETERNAL DAMNATION!

Warrior's Creed

I will not shake, I will not falter,
For more strength, I'll cling to the altar...
In courage I stand, with the Lord of Host,
In wisdom as the sea, I swim better than most...
With a fiery stare, I cast my vote,
For the enemy's folly, thus heathen I smote...
Like water for sand, I wash away filth,
Like an unseen power, I move with stealth...
I am a force unmatched, with the backing of Christ,
Here on the battlefield, I clear this heist...
I take up my sword, of diamond and gold,
I jump in first, toward the enemy I'm cold...
I clear a path, I take no spoil,
To disrupt this evil, I'm glad to foil...
On my left, stands an evil hoard,
From my right, I swing my deadly sword...
To watch as they cleave in two, I will not gloat,
Not even when I'm through...
I'll be in victory and sing for God,
I smile at Jesus, He gives a nod...
Christ my Saviour, gives new strategy,
My violence by force, I give no apology...
For evil a swift blow, a taste of love in God's sight,
Darkness can do nothing, against the Fathers might...
A warrior's spirit, that's what I've got, grace lending, the
Father willing, fire from Heaven, wax hot...
I have the power, from a Kingdom of old
Because of the Father, my faith is bold,
On Earth I have a backing, an army galore
In Heaven I'm a general, a show of might to explore...
A taste for vengeance, is not what I bore,

An act of justice, on this for more...
My shiny armor, of the holiest steel,
Welding a sword, from the highest mill...
A shield in hand, to block all evil,
With a shout from the Lord, for all soul's retrieval, with knowledge of the take back, I win with wisdom, For God's my source, my place in Freedom!

1st Thessalonians 2:4 (ESV)
But just as we have been approved by God to entrusted with the gospel, so we speak, not to please man, but to please God who test our hearts.

CHAPTER ONE

Revelations

"Neglect not the gift that is in thee…"
1 Timothy 4:14 (KJV)

"God has a Kingdom not an Empire, Satan has that, and an Empire is of a secular nature not of God!"
-BLS-

"I want to make a difference with people who want to make a difference doing something that makes a difference"
-John C. Maxwell-

Knowledge is power but having an open heart and mind to the signs and wonders of Christ is Powerful! This is my account on Heaven and Hell from all the dreams, visions and revelations I've had over the years with the most detail in the most real sense. But make no mistake, I have not been to either place! These visions and dreams of mine were almost like watching television about someone else and what that person was going through. That someone else was 'Me.' In my dreams, I had different encounters and experiences. Every event that I witnessed was so that I could understand in that spiritual level what I was operating in. So, in saying this from memory and by the Wisdom and Grace from God, I wrote this the best way that I could.

I have also added some of my views with opinions, my later dreams and revelations followed by some research and experiences throughout my life. People, Jesus is coming back for His Church, spotless and without wrinkle. We are the last generation before the return of Christ. We need to be ready, because I believe that this is the season for the return of the Lord. At an early age, I paid attention to my surroundings and noticed some things that my parents were trying to get me to understand. Years later, between the ages of seven to fifteen is when I started really listening and understanding. I still acted like a dumb kid without a care in the world, but I was also trying to hear what God was trying to say to me. To this day of writing this book, I have never heard the voice of God, but He still communicates with me through dreams.

Like many others, God (the Father of all Creation) has given me the gift of revelation for the spirit world. I can't explain it; I just have it. Although, being awake, I've never actually seen either angel or demon in the spirit world. I have seen more than enough demon activity whether on television or just in people! I have always tried to listen the best way that I could to understand how to. When you are a child with everything sparking your interest, it's pretty hard to pay attention especially when girls are present. Even though I acted as a child, I still had a heart reaching toward God. Many of my peers didn't feel this way because they were children, but I always did. These so-called people pretending to be adults would want to do wrong. As a child, I could see that it was wrong in some of the things they were doing. The sad thing was, some of these people were Christians. To ignore God is to accept Satan, there is no in-between. Either you want God, or you want the Devil. Any Rebellion against God opens a door for Satan to enter. So, be a good steward for the good things of God or else Satan will have his arms open to grab you. Remember, Rebellion is Witchcraft and that comes from Sheol!

It is always good practice to be proficient and professional even when you're relaxing by yourself, talking with people in simple communication, at any type of function or just out with friends and family. Whenever you're involved in any one of these, just know that because you are a child of the King of Kings, this puts you in a class of Royalty! Because of this respect, you will have a spotlight on you everywhere you go and in everything you say and do. You must hold yourself accountable in all actions and in all activities. Your integrity will always be questioned if you're not living the life of righteousness for righteousness sake.

Whatever you do can be taken out of context, and something positive you may have done can also by looked down upon because of jealously. If you're not living with God our Father in your own life, then you're automatically living with Satan our Enemy! You could say things in a joking manner and be offensive to others, but in your defense, everybody does it. Besides, you both would always joke around about any and everything, but one day it goes too far. You almost lost an excellent friendship, but because of the Holy Spirit in both of your lives, you both are still friends. Although, it isn't the same as before. Most outcomes do not turn out this way. It only takes one time for something negative to come about. For whatever reason it happens, it will to be changed forever, but sometimes not for the worst. Although, in any case, it won't be the same as it was before.

I don't care; however, most people would like to look at it. It is still true today, because it was true in the past and it is true for our future. If you're not living with God and having a real relationship with Him, then you're living with the Devil and having a relationship with him! This is a true statement, and in fact, some would argue that even though you're not living a lifestyle that involves or includes God the Father, that doesn't mean that you're living with Satan and indulging in the ways of the enemy. People, to have God is to know God without the influence of Satan, but to have Satan is to know Satan without the influence of God. The devil would have you believe in a subtle way that you can have God and Satan in your life simultaneously, but it is written that you cannot serve two masters! To know God is to say no to Satan, and to know Satan is to say no to God.

If you accept the devil into your own mind, your own heart or your own lifestyle, then that's when your own personal chaos begins. It will only get worse for you and your family or surroundings. The enemy will blind you so bad that you will only see chaos and long for a world without God our Father, Jesus His Son and the Holy Spirit.

Can you imagine a world without the One True God? It's coming sooner than you believe!!!

Satan is watching us intently. He watches our flesh, and he knows our weaknesses unless we rely on Jesus for strength and wisdom.

Satan has been defeated so many times. God has also given us the power to defeat Satan and his Empire! Now having said that, this doesn't mean that you can command Satan to go back to Sheol or Hell. That privilege is left up to God our Father in Heaven. **You do** have the power that God gives you to tell Satan to back off and to resist him, but you must be without sin to operate this way. Let me say it this way. If you are in a sinful lifestyle and you want Satan to back off or you try to resist him without seeking the Repentance from God our Father, it will not work because you're not wanting to do it the right way. It's like spitting in the wind without any protection of it coming back and hitting you in the face.

Jesus only told Satan to get behind Him and that It was written. When the body of Moses was disputed over, Satan was only rebuked with the power of God behind both Jesus and Michael.

Jude 1:9 (ESV)
"But when the archangel Michael, contending with the devil, was disputing about the body of Moses, he did not presume to

pronounce a blasphemous judgment, but said, "The Lord rebuke you."

Matthew 4:10 (ESV)

Then Jesus said to him, "Be gone, Satan! For it is written, You shall worship the Lord your God and him only shall you serve."

Revelation 12:7-12 (ESV)

"Now war arose in heaven, Michael and his angels fighting against the dragon. And the dragon and his angels fought back, but he was defeated, and there was no longer any place for them in heaven.

And the great dragon was thrown down, that ancient serpent, who is called the devil and Satan, the deceiver of the whole world-he was thrown down to the earth, and his angels were thrown down with him. And I heard a loud voice in heaven, saying, "Now the salvation and the power and the kingdom of our God and the authority of his Christ have come, for the accuser of our brothers has been thrown down, who accuses them day and night before our God.

And they have conquered him by the blood of the Lamb and by the word of their testimony, for they loved not their lives even unto death. Therefore, rejoice, O heavens and you who dwell in them! But woe to you, O earth and sea, for the devil has come down to you in great wrath, because he knows that his time is short!"

There are times, whether past or present, when I've heard something disturbing to my spirit and later finding out why or seeing things that haven't happened yet or having that strange feeling... "I've done this before!" There was this one situation that could've determined my friendship with one of the guys at the gym. But because I remembered the outcome, I used wisdom and kept a friend. Sometimes, God will place a burden on your heart for someone or a situation. When this happens, you must pray for whatever your burden is. No matter what time it is, you must pray. It could happen while you are asleep or wide awake. Whenever this happens, PRAY. if you Ignore it, something negative could happen all because of your disobedience.

I had a dream, and in this dream, I saw little pulsating purple lights barely visible coming in and going out on the ceiling. I had the impression that Heaven was coming down to us meaning that my family, my Wife and I were destroying the works of the enemy and the enemy himself. All of this happened around 2am. The name Angie popped into my mind, so I prayed for her. I haven't the slightest clue as to what the whole dream really meant, but God knows. When this happens, don't ever question God. Just pray whenever He tells you too! If we all used just a little bit of wisdom that God gave to us, we wouldn't be in as much trouble as we often get in to!

"I'm a good person"..."I'll go to Heaven"..."I'll do a good deed and the good will outweigh the bad"..."I really don't have to go to church to go to heaven," you ever heard any of those before? Sad to say that I've heard more than that. There are those who don't really have the slightest clue about what's really going on in the world. Seeing some people who might condone, or compromise demon activity just makes me sick to my stomach! When people sin, they believe some are better or worse than others; like a little white lie.

A Sin has no size comparison, a Sin has no precedence over another Sin, and a Sin isn't worse than another Sin. All Sins are equal to each other and can equally send you to Hell! A lie is the same as Bestiality. These are both Sins and these are both the same.

1 John 3:7 (ESV)
"Little children, let no one deceive you. Whoever practices righteousness is righteous, as he is righteous.

Luke 13:3 (ESV)
"No, I tell you; but unless you repent, you will all likewise perish."

Psalms 51:11 (ESV)
"Cast me not away from your presence and take not your Holy Spirit from me."

There are also some people who try to follow hard after a Christ like heart. But in a world filled with temptation and sin,…sometimes it feels utterly impossible. Sometimes you might feel like giving up! That's why when I see a diamond in the rough; for example, someone not giving in to sin but living for Christ and letting God work through them, it charges my spirit up! God is expecting you to use the arsenal of Heaven for parting the Red Sea in your life. He knows that you can't do it by yourself, so that's why He gives us the authority we need to move impossible odds. God wants you in Prosperity, and He wants you to progress towards your bright future. God is a Right Now God. If God expects you to do something, then you should expect God to move on your behalf, but you must be on the same page as God for this to work.

This is what gives me the strength to move a mountain all the while it warms my heart. Knowing that I'm not alone in spreading the Gospel of Christ which also gives me more zeal to carry on! Jesus crosses the lines of reality and impossibilities for us for our victory and all glory to God! Every year, you must Re-a-just yourself for a Renewal of your mind in Christ, a Rebalancing of your lifestyle with Christ and a Recalibration through Christ to stay on that straight and narrow. You know, it wouldn't hurt to do this on a regular either, like once a month or so. In my youth, I would often stop and reflect about what's happening all around me. With the knowledge of the spirit world in my head, there were always different thoughts or sounds that would come to me.

I would walk around (even to this day) and see people in their own little world, totally oblivious to the consequences they will face. Whether it's, not believing in an 'After Life,' or participating in things that can and willfully be damaging. In most cases, be damning to their very own soul; not to mention who else could fall just by following 'The in Crowd!'

Anyone who breathes air should be aware, or they could have someone else's blood on their own hands. Don't just take my word for it, read the Word of God and seek for understanding! Just a side note for you to realize. If you don't believe, then you get on your knees and pray, do your own research and involve Heavenly Wisdom in your findings. But if you really don't want to hear the truth or do your own research for the truth, then don't waste your time if you would rather be ignorant. Having said that, I've seen certain ones stop reading or going to Church just because they didn't like what was said. This is a good way to stay blinded by the enemy. At least, see where I am coming from. When I was a child, I thought as a child. But whenever I heard something that didn't sound right, I didn't just shut it down or stop listening. I did my own research and discovered the truth of what was being said or exposed something that was a farce.

Now understand, that people who participate in the Pagan Holiday which is known to all as Halloween is celebrating a satanic holiday. It doesn't matter if a party is put on by any type of church or just taking the kids on a harmless 'Trick or Treat.' In a Worldly theme, it's still celebrating a demon holiday (parties, candy, dressing up etc.). I know this sounds bad. By doing something that is against the Word of God and siding with what the World may do for any event which claims to be harmless fun, is detrimental to your spirit man. Not to mention, that it is also counterproductive to your growth as a Believer in Jesus Christ.

I understand that your child or children may be very young. Some that can walk and some that may not; 1 to 6 years. Please understand that you are placing yourself and your children into spiritual danger. You would be opening a door for the Horde of Hell to enter into your family's lives! Depending on how strong you are in Christ as the Blood falls over you and your family, the Bible says that we should not be ignorant of the devil's devices!

1 Corinthians 10:18-21 (ESV)

"Consider the people of Israel: are not those who eat the sacrifices participants in the altar? What do I imply then? That food offered to idols is anything, or that an idol is anything? No, I imply that what pagans sacrifice they offer to demons and not to God. I do not want you to be participants with demons. You cannot drink the cup of the Lord and the cup of demons. You cannot partake of the table of the Lord and the table of demons."

I will say this a few times so that you will understand, some of the referenced information that I found was not recorded when researched. As I went back for any referenced information, I could not find it, but new information was found and references from the newly acquired information was recorded.

Those that partake of Halloween in an innocent fashion are totally oblivious to the fact that they are open for an attack from the enemy. This kind of affliction starts naturally and ends spiritually. Thank God for His Amazing Grace lest we all perish from the curse! I'll mention this again later. An Ex Warlock which pastors a Church for the glory of God preaches the truth, and he tells it like it is on why we shouldn't celebrate Halloween or have any kind of celebration on the 31st or the week. Because in doing that, you are still opening up yourselves to an attack from the enemy. Churches that have celebrations on the same week or day of Halloween is still celebrating a demon holiday, even if these churches change the name to a friendlier childlike name. Even at that, the children are still allowed to dress up in costumes. It's so dangerous spiritually.

I did some digging on Halloween and found a little history for you. Did you know that before Halloween, there was a celebration around the same time as the Pagan Holiday? It was an actual 'Harvest Party.' This Harvest was celebrated by Egyptians. I'm sure that the dressing up followed by the candy was just perverted by the devil, because the Egyptians wore makeup and jewelry with an abundance of meat, fruit and vegetables. Where in far off lands, Monks would put on ceremonial robes, travel in a group through a village and stop at some one's home then say in their own native tongue which is translated to us as "Trick or Treat!" The trick was asking for a virgin (candy), but if they were refused, the treat was everyone being brutally slaughtered, and the virgin taken anyway. No one in her family was spared.

Although, the Egyptians always worshiped gods, they were also flawed without the one true God. Those Druids were evil, and they worshiped demons, but would also wear masks and costumes to represent demons so they wouldn't be possessed. That is what you celebrate when October 31st comes, hence the name Halloween taken from 'Old Hallows Eve!' Again, if you don't believe me read your history...you'd be amazed at what you'll find, if it's still there.

Some of the information that I researched before writing this wasn't recorded, so I didn't get the references. After going back to acquire these references, I could not find them.

I'm not trying to get anyone upset. I'm just trying to get your attention and get you to open your eyes, for those of you who walk around with their eyes wide shut! Although, in my opinion, anything that is 'Done in Fun' on Halloween means you're just supporting an evil cause, unless the celebration is focused on the Harvest and not during the same week or day as Halloween! The children are our first concern by keeping them safe, because the Enemy wants our children and our children are our future. We all need to look at the bigger picture here. Whatever we do here on Earth (the natural realm) is also affected in the spiritual realm whether good or bad. We should always keep our focus on the children; Satan does. The spiritual applications attached to whatever activities that we participate in can be negative to our spirit-man, if the participation is in anything that doesn't include God our Father. This is a fact that is overlooked by most, especially Christians.

This is what I'm used to. Whatever day Halloween fell on, my family and I would be at either prayer followed by fellowship, a bible study followed by fellowship, church followed by fellowship, having fellowship or just relaxing at home as if this where just another day. We wouldn't be giving out candy or hiding in the dark. I know it sounds rude, but when you know and follow the truth, this World and its actions will be nothing to you! I did some more research on this, and that is what I found but once again. Later going back to reference my work, I couldn't find most of it anywhere. However, I did find more back history on this subject out of **Wikipedia, History.com** and **the University of Albany.** Even though this information seemed incomplete, I was satisfied with my results.

The Assistant Professor in the Department of Folklore and Mythology at UCLA said that the Celtic festival known as 'Samhain' (Sow-in, Sow-een, Shahvin, Samhuin, Samhuinn) is the earliest trace of Halloween before the name changed from Samhain, which is also the

Celtic New Year and marks the summers end. This was the ending of summer and the beginning of winter.

This was a dark time that meant human deaths. The druids danced around bon fires and wore costumes dressed of animal heads, witches, ghosts and goblins, because they believed that they wouldn't get possessed if they looked like a demon. When our Christian children go out in demon custom look-a-like costumes, even if they go out looking like angels or royalty, our children are doing the same thing as the early Druids and we are allowing it to happen. When Christian parents aren't listening to what God has said about certain things, then there is a problem.

I understand if you just didn't know, but also remember that in Jesus' day, their children had fun without the Pagan festivities. If people knew just what was going on in the spiritual realm around the Halloween time period, then they wouldn't even let their children go out trick or treating. There was a movie that I watched as a teenager called, 'From Beyond.' It was about a psychiatrist and scientist testing an invention made from a deceased inventor for the purposes of stimulating the pineal gland. Doing this brought about another dimension. Whenever this machine was turned on, it made what was invisible visible.

In this movie, you could see what was all around you just by the machine being on and running. But whenever it was switched off, you could see nothing as if it never happened. Even though you couldn't see it anymore, those things swimming around you were still there. Now, as in the Spirit Realm, you can't see what's swimming or walking around you. So even as a movie, this is an actual reality of what is going on in the Spirit Realm.

Instead of things swimming around you, depending on if you have the precious Blood of the Lamb covering you, your family, your finances and your things, whatever you can't see around you could be Angels or Demons. This is our reality in whatever we do, whether we are in the presence of the Heavenly Host or the presence of the Enemy.

What's walking or swimming around you if you are in sin or the presence of the Holy Spirit?

There was this one minister that I briefly recall that could see demons all around people; small and large. In some areas, the demons were the size of small chimpanzees, and in other areas they were much larger. I was listening to Pastor, Evangelist and Teacher, Dr. Perry Stone when I heard this. There are Angels, demons and other things all around us that we can't see, so we need to be careful in what we touch or allow in our lives. Every little thing that is done in the celebration of Halloween is against Heaven and being against Heaven isn't where you need to be. This origin of Halloween goes back for centuries and in 43 A.D., the Romans took occupation over Celtic territory. The Romans had their own festivals, two of them as a matter of fact. First(1st) was the Feralia which was the passing of the dead, and Second(2nd) was the Day for honoring Pomona, the Roman goddess of fruits and trees.

In 835 A.D., Pope Gregory IV substituted the name, 'All Saints Day' as it spread throughout Europe. Christian village children did the Danse Macabre in celebration of All Saints Day. Seven (7) people died as the result of dressing up in demon costumes, these deaths are described in the Seventh (7th) chapter of the Deuterocanonical book of

Second (2nd) Macabees. These articles go on and get worse. The World is compromising and cloaking the truth, and Satan wants us to forget our history and has no cares for the truth; just lies! If people knew the truth or even cared about this gruesome history, I believe there would be a change in people's lives. Forgive me if I sound like 'Fire and Brimstone,' but this needs to be said. People need to know the truth no matter how it sounds. If people are concerned about their own souls, something must be done!

Some people think that if they are a good person in life, they're Heaven bound, but as the truth is revealed, I'm sorry to say, that they are really Hell bound. I do feel sorry for anyone who thinks in this manner, because until they allow God to do His work and not tie His hands...they really will be Hell Bound! The **ONLY WAY** to get to Heaven is to be **SAVED** by **JESUS CHRIST!**

Too many people get swayed by Worldly ways or join crazy religions trying to find something to fill the void in their life when the simplest thing to do is look up. Some are so bull headed that they only want to do it their own way.

The ones who don't believe in God the Father are in for a shock. He sure believes in them, but then again so does Satan. If this fallen angel can make more people believe that there's no God, then they would forget about Him and be Worldly which places them far from Heaven and closer to Hell! There are so many different temptations or other trivial things that might slip in knowingly or unknowingly. That's why we all as individuals and as a body in Christ must stay close to the Holy Trinity. It is very important that we also surround ourselves with others that are Holy Ghost filled whether it being relationships or friendships! You must be Equally Yoked, and you both need to be on the same page, so to speak. You both should operate on the same level. What the Father God puts together, let no man or demon undo. This isn't in the Bible, but there are similar scriptures in there.

What does Divorce really mean? To Force a Division between something that is whole. What does Marriage really mean? To form a Unique Relationship between God, and Man and Woman into a Perfect Union; to bring together the Unity of One Flesh.

Is it any wonder why divorce has a two-part meaning and marriage has a one part meaning; these meanings couldn't be on accident! Since Adam and Eve, Satan has tried to tear marriage apart. Even though he can't, he will continue to try. There are other ways that he will explore like throwing Christians off the beaten path in many ways like something you'd never expect. In Church sermons, some of the teacher's speech is off. Either it's because of a speech impediment or it's because they're saying the word wrong. These actions do not make any sense to me at all, from giving a false or twisted message to pronouncing a word wrong on purpose. What happened to the common sense and wisdom that God has given us? Have some of us rather leave our senses behind and look dumb in front of people or am I picking at something that doesn't really matter?

I wouldn't mention this if I hadn't of seen or heard this take place over a period, so this means that I have witnessed these events take place. I will say that I have noticed people with good educations speaking as though they are without proper training in education. They know better; that's the sad part! It's crazy! But when some people do this, it brings others down and unless these people are strong enough in the Lord God, then something like speech won't bring them down.

I don't understand why some people would say a word wrong on purpose when it comes off as that person looking like someone who is ignorant but in a strange way, they think they're special. I guess that could be the reason why, but I hear it more often than I'd like to comment on. The sad thing is that I also hear it from educated men and women which doesn't make sense to me. I understand speech impediments, lisps or old age. But when there's nothing wrong with a person's speech and they choose to say a word wrong so they can sound cool or special, then that's a real problem. This sort of action doesn't come from God; it comes from the enemy. You see, Satan wants us to go backwards in our learning. He doesn't want us to move forward, and when people do this, they take away from what they could be learning.

In a subtle way, our education system would be moving backwards. If you move backwards, you could cause yourself to become unstable in your thinking. Many people would say that I'm overreacting. I remember when I was in high school, and I knew this kid that played the saxophone in the Marching Band. He would play the wrong notes on purpose. I asked him why he would always do that, and he said that he liked doing it. He added that he didn't know why he did it, but he would see if he could get something started. He wanted to see if he could start a new fad, and he didn't care if people thought he was weird. That kid wanted a following. He was just a kid with hardly the education of a scholar but acting as a child having harmless fun. **What's their problem?**

Most of these people have multiple degrees and doctorates in their names, but they still insist on pronouncing a word wrong. Doesn't make much sense to me why they do it, but they do. I've seen a Pastor do that and the men in his Church follow him by also pronouncing words wrong. It was something that they did, and it didn't make sense to me, but it didn't take away from my learning, listening and meditating on the Word of God. I will say that while they all did this, I did notice that the move of the Holy Spirit, within the walls of that Church dwindled down. By saying that, if other people are paying attention to their mispronunciations and it bothers them so much that they get distracted, they could lose their footing and fall off the narrow path. I believe that is one of the enemy's plan for disintegrating humanity; especially Christians. Satan is trying to distract us into looking into another direction even for a moment. This is enough to throw us off track completely and have movement in a place that isn't meant for us to be in. Most people would believe that what I'm saying is a STRETCH, and there are those that would have you to believe that these words are nonsense. God our Father wants us to prosper while Satan wants us to fail.

In a Marriage, there needs to be 5 things that will guarantee a long and successful life together. 1st. There should always be communication with God the Father and between Husband and Wife. 2nd. There needs to be an obligation to God then to each other before anyone and anything else; especially in a Brand-New Marriage. If either person is putting another person, event, financial situations, Church activities or children ahead of their spouse or God or both, your marriage together will suffer and then sometimes fail! 3rd. One spouse should always have the back of the other.

4th. The Husband should always take the leadership role and be a good steward for the Kingdom of God. It is always good to remember that if the Man of the house isn't doing what he is supposed to do in the eyes of God, then God will raise up the Woman of the house to get things done and taken care of in order to save what He has put together. It may look as if the Wife will rule over the Husband, but only in his mind will he think this. Until he can get his act together, this will happen. 5th. Both Husband and Wife should always keep God first in their Marriage and use Heavenly Wisdom. It's very important to keep God in the forefront of your marriage. These five things are crucial when expecting a successful future with God, your spouse, your family, your finances and your financial obligations. The Men need to act accordingly to their responsibilities as husband, father and Man of the house. Communication is the main key to a successful marriage!

I say these things because it is true, and I have seen this happen before my very eyes. You can't make this up!

Now for those who are married to an unbeliever, there is hope! You see, it is in the Lord's plan to see you through it all. The person you're with is either going to get saved or God the Father is showing you something important while that person you've married is seeing the truth being exposed for the first time in their life. You are a gift to him or her and to their family.

Take heed for your life together will try your own faith, and Satan will try to break up your marriage followed by your faith and destroy your joy then your soul! What about if you think that you're in love and get married, but your spouse changed colors after the fact? That is another trick of the enemy, because Satan knew you were weak. Yet, there is still hope. God has a plan for your life, so never give up even when it looks impossible. God didn't tell you to marry an unbeliever, that's being unequally yoked. If you are unequally yoked anyway, now you are beating your head up against a wall. Again, don't worry because God has your back. Even when one person of another Faith, Religion or Denomination catches your eye, beware of a Jezebel Spirit in your mist!

Psalms 1:1-6 (ESV)

"Blessed is the man who walks not in the counsel of the wicked, nor stands in the way of sinners, nor sits in the seat of scoffers; but his delight is in the law of the LORD, and on his law he meditates day and night. He is like a tree planted by streams of water that yields its fruit in its season, and its leaf does not wither. In all that he does, he prospers. The wicked are not so, but are like chaff that the wind drives away. Therefore, the wicked will not stand in the judgment, nor sinners in the congregation of the righteous; for the LORD knows the way of the righteous, but the way of the wicked will perish."

What if you are married to someone with a wondering eye or likes to flirt a lot but it's not with you, what does this mean? Men and women that cheat on their spouses have been deceived by the wiles of the enemy.

There are certain guidelines to follow or ideas to think about...

1. You disrespect God our Father; you're offending Jesus and you can possibly blaspheme the Holy Spirit!

2. You disrespect your spouse causing a spiritual rift to form within your family.

3. You disrespect the person that you are cheating with if they have a family causing a spiritual rift to form within the walls of their family.

4. You disrespect the spouse's spouse, the person that you are cheating with on your spouse, which is the same for them because they are also cheating on their own spouse as well. So, you are disrespecting their spouse.

5. You are now labeled as a liar, cheat and coward.

6. You caused an irreversible situation to come about, and because of it, a family is now torn apart.

7. You didn't use Wisdom. Courageous behavior is no longer what people see in you anymore.

8. You have just played into the hands of the enemy.

9. You have just opened the door to the enemy and now a generational curse is in your family tree.

10. You now have a decision to make. Will you repeat your actions, or will you repent of your actions and come back to Christ?

For anyone who has these issues and are trying to live for Jesus Christ, this is written for you. For the non-believers that are going through the unfortunate events of cheating, this isn't meant for you because you are at the mercy of the enemy and not God! If you are in any of those situations, you need to stay strong and stay close to God! The Bible says that we should not be Unequally Yoked. If we are blinded by ourselves, there is still hope in Jesus Christ! There are three discoveries that you should know of, if you are to follow the ways of Jesus Christ. 1) God loves you. 2) You are in Gods Family and 3) God's Purpose for your life. It is our duty and responsibility to show the love of God to all, not just Christ like people. So, we should not ever judge others or else we'll be judged!

God loves you, so you should show the love of God to others. We are in one great big family of God. If Satan can cause a division within us, he can conquer us easily. Therefore, we need to stay close to the Holy Trinity. Satan wants to confuse us into believing in chaos as real truth, and we should always look out for each other because Satan wants control over us. He hates us and wants us dead. Because of the protection of God over us, Satan can't touch us unless we fall out of the family of God. Our purpose in life is to spread the Gospel of Jesus Christ to the World, if we choose too. Choosing the family of God is where His protection is. You are surrounded by Jesus and the Kingdom of Heaven. Choosing outside of the family of God is to automatically choose Satan and the Empire of Hell which is in control of this World. I keep saying Empire instead of Kingdom, because I don't believe that Hell has the privilege of being called a Kingdom, only Heaven!

I believe that our history is divided into 3 acts: Perfect Laws, Desolation and Restoration. Those that are Rotten on the inside have no God in them, and they've rejected or cast away the Word of God which is also Law. Everything in this Universe operates in Laws. If you break a law, there are consequences; the same goes for the spiritual. If you break any laws in the spirit realm, there are consequences; one always follows the other. Satan wants you to feel defeated, alone, no hope, confused, vulnerable and gullible to the Empire of Hell.

Satan wants you to feel like God can't forget your sins and that He won't let you be happy. One of Satan's greatest tools is Shame. Satan needs you to believe that God won't forgive you because of your sins. If you are a friend of emptiness and destruction, you will easily be preyed upon with misery and despondency from Satan. You will be in such a powerful state of desolation where only the absolute power of the precious Blood of the Lamb can set you free, but you must want to be saved. God has unlimited chances if you're trying to get it right with Him unless you reject Him or you yourself give up! You're never too far gone unless it's your choice to long for wicked things instead of things that are Holy.

You don't want anything to do with Satan, especially sin. Whenever you sin, you have something in common with Satan. In the beginning, Satan sinned and regarding your own sin, you have sin in common with Satan. The Restoration of Jesus Christ for your eternal soul is your only way to freedom, and that is just the beginning to Heavenly Freedom. There are many steps in the wrong direction, but one step back towards the Father and that road is only as tough as you make it to be.

"The journey of 1000 miles starts with the 1st step"
I'll probably mention this again, but what about Laws vs Grace?

What is the difference between laws and grace? Laws and grace should always be balanced because they are equal in balance! When the pharisees caught the adulteress in the sexual act, I believe that it was premeditated; on the pharisees end. What I mean by that is, they knew what was going on behind closed doors. They waited until it was done, so they could bring forth damaging information to trap Jesus in an unlawful action in a disgraceful manner. They wanted to see if Jesus would contend law and grace or law versus grace.

The pharisees grabbed the woman and brought her to Jesus. What about the man that they supposedly caught her with? I believe that it was probably one of them with the woman to set Jesus up. It was never really about the woman and the fact that these evil misguided men would kill this woman by stoning her is sickening. She was just collateral damage. The reason why they brought her to Jesus was to try to trap Him into an unlawful action of presenting law verse grace. Now, if they had of known in their hearts and minds that Jesus was balanced in everything, they would never have brought that woman to Him. When they brought her to Jesus, He made them all look as though they all had a lack of intelligence without an ounce of common sense. When they all dropped their stones, their agenda was shattered once again. The woman was set free without sin and with forgiveness!

Coming up as a child, I learned as a child and as a man, I am still learning what God our Father is showing me. I am being led by the Holy Spirit of God and I am allowing Jesus to guide me through troubled waters. I am discovering the different truths about Tithes and Offerings, the differences of Living and Surviving, dissecting the scriptures and understanding the deeper meanings of the Word of God. I am also learning how to pull down Strong Holds which comes directly from ourselves! Finally, I now understand the differences between Laws, Grace and Righteousness.

Grace and RIGHTEOUSNESS are being confused with each other. Grace without righteousness becomes frustrated grace while righteousness is being forgotten and grace is being overlooked. Grace and Righteousness are sacred. Now a days, when grace is being taught in some Churches, the congregation, for the most part, are still sinning because of the belief that God will have grace over you when you sin. It's the belief of When You Sin! The Grace of God is only if you sin and want a change of heart and mind to the ways of God our Father; not a matter of whenever you sin without a chance of change.

God doesn't work that way. If He did, then you could call Him a liar and God is incapable of lies, God cannot sin! God our Father of all Creation sent His only begotten Son, Jesus Christ to die on the Cross at the hill they called a Skull for the remission of our sins. This beloved action saved us all (humanity) from sin and death. You must choose the Straight and Narrow, so you won't have to see Hell. So, here's my question for all the ones who keeps on Sinning and is loving Worldly ways instead of Godly ways of Righteousness...If you Love God, then why don't you stop doing that sinful nature of things and accept Jesus into your heart?

If you love God, then stop sinning!

2 Chronicles 7:14 (ESV)

"If my people who are called by my name humble themselves, and pray and seek my face and turn from their wicked ways, then I will hear from heaven and will forgive their sin and heal their land."

This is how we all should be. In the scripture stating that we humble ourselves, God was directly speaking to the Church, the Believers; not the Nonbeliever or Secular Community. God expects us, the Church to bring the Gospel of Jesus Christ to the Nonbeliever for his or her own Salvation so that they will be Saved!

God wasn't talking about the secular community or society; He was talking to the Church....it's a Church Call to be Humble!

All of our Sins confessed and un-confessed have been forgiven by God, but it doesn't mean that we can still Sin. Most adults who go through problems know why they go through these situations but would rather do it their own way other than the right way and then they wonder why they fail so easily. A stronghold in your life is strong enough to cause your flesh to overrule the wisdom that you are supposed to have. This wisdom is what God has given you. If you ignore it, then you give strength to your flesh, ultimately your stronghold. To pull down this stronghold, you need the help of Jesus. Ask Jesus to help you and stay strong in your own pursuit of pulling down your own strongholds. Don't give up or in, because the more you resist your own flesh, the closer you will receive your Breakthrough!

It is important to know that without Jesus you cannot cast out a stronghold. A stronghold could be in the form of Bitterness,

Unforgiveness, etc. etc. Strongholds can be many different things. Bitterness and Unforgiveness are signs of a broken soul refusing to remain broken. If you can't be broken for God to mend you, then your bitterness and unforgiveness will be a very strong stronghold in your life just to mention a few. The blessings that you receive from God is just a product of your faith.

What does your faith produce?

What is the productivity of your faith?

Does your Faith lay dormant and wait for something to happen, or are you pro-active in receiving from God and producing your faith much bigger than what it was before?

Whenever you move in the direction that God wants, things will happen in your favor; build your faith and God will build you. Pastor and Evangelist, Jesse Duplantis said, "Your financial prosperity for tomorrow will be determined by your obedience today." This is true for the building of your future with Jesus leading, and God prospering you to great and excellent ways. Although, some people would actually disagree with this true statement; any disagreement that goes against what God our Father wants to do for us is Folly. It doesn't make much sense to me.

There are people who believe what they say is true, but they're off track in ways that will send them completely over into the wrong way of thinking. They have strong feelings about what they are saying or doing, and their actions are not for God but against what His Word says and means. These people have Strong Holds in their lives, deeply rooting itself inside their own hearts and minds. These same people do not even see because of the blinders they have placed over their own eyes.

Ever since I could remember, as a little boy, I'd watch my parents' worship in church and be blessed from their own faithfulness. Now, as I grow older, my worship is not just in church, but in everything I do and everywhere I go; just as my parents did...to this day. Sure, as a human, I often fall surrounded by all kinds of temptations. But if I don't get back up and dust myself off, I'll end up giving Satan all victory; and that goes for anybody! In my past, I never did really study the Bible, but I still have a strong love for the Word of God and my desire for a deeper relationship with Him grows more every day. I can't get enough of the Word of God. I want to learn more. I want more of Him!

Seven Habits that are excellent to have are....
1. **Feeding yourself on the Word of God**
2. **Developing a habit of a Prayer Life**
3. **Developing strong Worship and Praise**
4. **Developing a habit of Fellowship**
5. **Getting into the habit of Giving**
6. **Practice Serving**
7. **Disciple Making**

This is good practice which makes for an excellent perfection in Christ.

Coming up as a child, I'd often stop and reflect on many things like my life as well as my future. Then after a bit, I'd go resume playing or whatever it was I was doing. Even to this day, I always put God first in my life even though as a child I acted like I belonged in a zoo. Even now, I sometimes act as though common sense passed me by, but nevertheless, God is always first in my life!

I played Football in high school with the ugliest position stance, but I was good and getting better after each day of practice and every game day. I was giving all praise and glory to God. When you give God complete praise, glory and honor in whatever it is you're doing, then you will get the victory. I was doing very well on the football field. One day during my senior year, I was asked by one of my teammates on how I did so well. I told him everything on how to succeed as a football player like I was doing, and that he couldn't go wrong if he followed the same suit, but I was wrong, SO WRONG!

I didn't tell him what was supposed to be said…. God will always deserve the glory; it doesn't belong to us…. EVER! I should have said that instead, it's because of God that I was doing so well. I didn't acknowledge our Father, instead I let pride take the wheel, and then I took the glory from God and placed it on myself. Without the presence, protection and wisdom of God during that time in my life, I would've been just like any other kid trying to play sports. I wasn't really that good at it, but with God, I was excelling to great levels. I gave God the glory every time I stepped on the field, whether it was football practice or games. I gave God all the glory until that day. I've had a lot of heart ache since that time. I went through a lot of hurt both physically and emotionally; then spiritual pain followed. Always give God the glory.

Don't take it for yourself. In the Bible, didn't someone else do that? He didn't get what he was promised because of that glory stealing. I speak from experience. It doesn't feel good losing something before you can touch it all because you didn't use wisdom.

There was a time when I had so much zeal that I didn't know how to act until I had my first understanding about Hell. Every time, I'd see someone I knew that wasn't saved or just riding the fence, I could see that person burning in Hell! This image invaded my mind, and I could see the anguish in their face as they yelled at me; **"Why didn't you tell me about this!"**

I then saw their blood on my hands. I was to be held accountable, and my heart was grieved. This was very uncharacteristic in nature to see people burning in Hell; that's when I started focusing on major events like the End Times as well as Heaven and Hell. Soon after that, I started having Revelations from my Dreams and Visions.

I've had some visions beforehand and didn't understand them. The very first revelation from my dream I had was about the Rapture; taken from the Greek terminology and translated from "A Catching Away." This was brought to my attention right after I had the thought of, 'I have enough time to get my life right,' and then I saw myself being left behind but in a world with no God is unspeakable.

These visions just started flooding my mind, but the uncanny part was...I remembered everyone, and it's been over some years. I remember this one dream I had that woke me up out of a deep sleep. It was about some type of beast with a stinger. If it stung you, your pain would last for up to five months...Your Pain! **AND YOU COULDN'T DIE FROM IT!!!**

Revelation 9:1-21 (ESV)

"And the fifth angel blew his trumpet, and I saw a star fallen from heaven to earth, and he was given the key to the shaft of the bottomless pit. He opened the shaft of the bottomless pit, and from the shaft rose smoke like the smoke of a great furnace, and the sun and the air were darkened with the smoke from the shaft. Then from the smoke came locusts on the earth, and they were given power like the power of scorpions of the earth. They were told not to harm the grass of the earth or any green plant or any tree, but only those people who do not have the seal of God on their foreheads. They were allowed to torment them for five months, but not to kill them, and their torment was like the torment of a scorpion when it stings someone.

And in those days people will seek death and will not find it. They will long to die, but death will flee from them. In appearance the locusts were like horses prepared for battle: on their heads were what looked like crowns of gold; their faces were like human faces, their hair like women's hair, and their teeth like lions' teeth; they had breastplates like breastplates of iron, and the noise of their wings was like the noise of many chariots with horses rushing into battle.

They have tails and stings like scorpions, and their power to hurt people for five months is in their tails. They have as king over them the angel of the bottomless pit. His name in Hebrew is Abaddon, and in Greek he is called Apollyon. The first woe has passed; behold, two woes are still to come. Then the sixth angel blew his trumpet, and I heard a voice from the four horns of the golden altar before God, saying to the sixth angel who had the trumpet, "Release the four angels who are bound at the great river Euphrates."

So, the four angels, who had been prepared for the hour, the day, the month, and the year, were released to kill a third of mankind. The number of mounted troops was twice ten thousand times ten thousand; I heard their number. And this is how I saw the horses in my vision and those who rode them: they wore breastplates the color of fire and of sapphire and of sulfur, and the heads of the horses were like lions' heads, and fire and smoke and sulfur came out of their mouths.

By these three plagues a third of mankind was killed, by the fire and smoke and sulfur coming out of their mouths. For the power of the horses is in their mouths and in their tails, for their tails are like serpents with heads, and by means of them they wound. The rest of mankind, who were not killed by these plagues, did not repent of the works of their hands nor give up worshiping demons and idols of gold and silver and bronze and stone and wood, which cannot see or hear or walk, nor did they repent of their murders or their sorceries or their sexual immorality or their thefts."

Whenever the Rapture happens, life as we know it stops. Just before the Rapture, life is in a continuation from the day before, but you should realize that we are the Last Generation before the Rapture happens. We are in the season of the great Catching Away and the bringing of Hell on Earth without God. Note: Rapture is from the Greek translation of "A Catching Away!"

Be ready, in season and out! Watch what you put into your spirit. Something so innocent could be the very thing that will get you Left Behind! Movies, Television shows, Reality shows, U-Tube videos, Board games, Card games and games in general are subject to be a distraction from the things of God. Things that most of us think are harmless can be Television shows. Maybe not the shows itself, but who is Directing, Producing, Hosting or Endorsing, etc... etc... Whomever is a Homosexual, a Satanist, deals into Witchcraft or Voodoo, a Murderer, an Atheist, an Agnostic or anything that isn't of God, you should not watch because you take an awful risk of being under the influence of that enemy. A dangerous transference of evil into your mind.

If you open the door to the enemy, the enemy will come in like a flood and will cause you so much chaos in your life which can affect your decision making and ultimately confuse your identity in Christ. If you open a door to the enemy, the enemy will not only come in, but the enemy will cause more chaos than you can imagine unless you let Jesus have free reign into your life. Satan will distort your efforts to be clean of filth. If you're struggling without any progress towards God and His help, then your simple complex sin will become a chaotic complex sin with degradation.

Satan will entice you with sexual pleasures. He will make you believe that you can gratify yourself if no one is around. If Satan can get you to focus on yourself and not the Holy Spirit, then he can get you to sin against your own body. Self-gratification is not something that pleases God. In fact, that grieves the Holy Spirit, which is God, but so many people are justifying self-gratifying themselves. This and other activities are sinful with a stench to the nostrils of God. Too many people are compromising faith with fairness and Agape Love with Humanitarian Love. Too many people are making excuses and justifications for their actions in lustful activities, adultery, masturbation, taking drugs, smoking or drinking. It's wrong to do it period, because our bodies are not our own. Our bodies belong to God our Father!

The people in this world and of a Worldly Nature would rather do whatever they want whenever they want to themselves or to whomever they want; without repercussions. The sad thing is that some of the Christians today are condoning the same thing and justifying these wicked ways. That's why I don't refer to myself or others who are greater than I who walk in the ways of the Father God and allow the Holy Spirit to manifest Himself without any limitations throughout their lives as a Christian. But in a much better definition, a True Believer in Christ Jesus or a Disciple of Jesus Christ! I'm a Disciple of Jesus Christ in training. The Church embedded with today's society is adopting and justifying these sins as something tolerable. **SIN SHOULD NEVER BE TOLERATED!** But unfortunately, it is.

I'LL SAY IT AGAIN, SIN SHOULD NEVER BE TOLERATED!

Most Churches that I hear or know about don't really preach on sexual sins, but instead would rather preach a feel good or prosperity message. The congregation in any Church should be taught on topics that they should flee from, pray against and whenever possible, spread the good news of Jesus Christ where knowing and accepting the truth will set many free. Today's Churches in general do not know or really care to see about anything that has to do with matters of Fornication, Adultery, Homosexuality, Sodomy, Prostitution and Masturbation, but let's talk about self-gratification and discuss the others later.

(In General) The Church today has 3 Views on Masturbation:
   1. It is always Sinful, (They got this one right)
   2. It is only Sinful if you Lust, (They missed it)
   3. It is Always Acceptable, (They missed it) ...

Self-Gratification is just one mentioned here. A person's wicked lifestyle is a big one. The problem with most churches today is that they are more interested in filling up their pocketbooks and having sold out memberships, instead of saving more souls for the Kingdom of God and taking care of their flock. Many topics are left out and more prosperity messages are taught in certain ways to teach the congregation in a subtle way to give till it hurts. Many topics that I will cover later in this book will be explained. Make no mistake in what I say, not every Church is like this. Prosperity messages are excellent topics when taught right and understood. It can be dangerous if you leave out God our Father, and Jesus Christ His Son from any message that is to be taught within the walls of Church. It states in the Bible that serving both God and money isn't tolerated, Matthew 6:24.

Matthew 6:24 King James Version (KJV)

"No man can serve two masters: for either he will hate the one and love the other; or else he will hold to the one and despise the other. Ye cannot serve God and mammon."

King James Version (KJV) Public Domain

I was listening to John Paul Jackson one day, and he mentioned in one of his sermons that a young man had a prophetic dream and he told his Pastor about it. The Pastor of that Church told this young man after hearing his dream that God doesn't give power like that, and that his dream wasn't from God, but the Pastor was wrong. His dream was from God. The young man left the Church never to return. But before he left, he said to the Pastor that he was going to find the one that gave him this dream and get that power he was supposed to have. This Pastor was wrong and ran off an Influential Man for the Kingdom of God.

This sort of thing happens a lot to young people with talents for the Kingdom of Heaven. Because of narrow-minded Pastors or Board Members, these kids with God given talents are snatched up by the enemy and they are used for the Empire of Hell. That young man became a Powerful Witch with a lot of influence. So, many are lost in sin, but praise be to God, there is redemption for their sins! You must be careful in whatever you watch because of Negative Spiritual Applications that can sneak into your Spirit-Man, if you watch reality shows, talk shows, the news, television shows and movies in which each one can be defective to your spirit in different ways. For example, an adulteress lifestyle that is overlooked, because everyone on the show is in sin. Someone that is in a homosexual lifestyle is overlooked, because sinful natures aren't frowned upon but in subtle ways, True Believers in Jesus are frowned upon because of their beliefs.

Shows that condone Adultery, Homosexuality, Witchcraft, Murder without remorse and heavy Curse Words are things that will infiltrate your Spirit and cause confusion in many areas in your everyday life. We should not watch these because these shows are not from God but from Hell. Why would you want to watch something that will cause chaos in your life?

Can you imagine if Jesus came back while you were watching something by someone or company that you shouldn't be watching because it is damaging to your Spirit-Man. Playing a game that you know is bad, but you justify in your own mind that it's fine. Maybe you're doing something that you know is wrong and against the teachings of God our Father, but you somehow reason within yourself that you will be forgiven of it; **then you are Left Behind! How does that make you feel? How does that make you look?** One of the main purposes of Satan is to desensitize you little by little so that you won't have any problem looking at or participating in sin.

I went to see a movie with a few friends from Church. This was going to be a good movie, or so we thought. This movie was called 'Noah,' and the only thing they got right about this movie was the name. This movie was between The Lord of the Rings, Conan the Barbarian, Gladiator alongside Babylonian times and Sodom and Gomorrah from biblical days. People that didn't know any better or just didn't care, thought that this was a good movie. Some thought it was accurate.

Movies or television shows with content like this are damaging to the spirit-man. God knows if you know and if you don't. God will let you know the Season of the Return of Christ before it's too late, because He loves you! **Don't mis-understand me, the season of His return is not the same as the hour.** The season is the understanding of knowing it's almost time of the return of Jesus for the gathering of His Church without spot or wrinkle.

In another one of my visions, I saw myself with some of my cousins hiding from the government. This other vision just blew my mind. I was in a church with some of its members and the Pastor of the church. In the horror of it all, we all realized that we were left behind!

Luke 19:42-44 (ESV)

"Saying, "Would that you, even you, had known on this day the things that make for peace! But now they are hidden from your eyes. For the days will come upon you, when your enemies will set up a barricade around you and surround you and hem you in on every side and tear you down to the ground, you and your children within you.

And they will not leave one stone upon another in you, because you did not know the time of your visitation."

In all my dreams, visions and revelations, I could feel the situation. After having these revelations about Heaven and Hell, I had yet another Vision. I was lying face up on the ground when I opened my eyes to a world filled with excellence. As I sat up, there was this warm feeling that came over me. I started walking around checking out the area when this huge eagle landed right in front of me. It had a wingspan like two small automobiles with the most powerful looking beak. Just the sight of this magnificent creature sent chills up and down my spine, but I was unafraid.

The Eagle wanted me to follow him without uttering a word. I took in a quick glance around and as far as my eye could see there was land flourished with trees, mountains, hills, vegetation, streams, rivers and an ocean, YES... AN OCEAN! Anyway, I looked up noticing there above the clouds was a ceiling. I was dumbfounded, next thing I knew I was in the air...Flying! I thought to myself, 'How this could be possible?' The eagle that was in flight ahead of me shifted left and disappeared underneath the water. I followed and found myself under water also. I saw life, some of which I'd never seen before. The eagle was again in front of me, so I followed the Eagle. As we flew up from the water, I again looked around and saw more life. There were animals both under water and on land. Flying upwards, I focused on this amazing ceiling. As I flew closer, I noticed behind the clouds there was an opening, or for lack of a better word...a hole. I approached this opening, but an opening to where?

I took a last look around and flew in, but wherever the Eagle disappeared to, I have no clue. The walls within this hole as I flew up looked almost organic. Then as I was going up, I hit what looked like another opening to a cave or a series of tunnels that took me right then up then left then up. After doing this for a while, I came to yet another opening, so I started traveling up. As I flew upwards, there was a sound that grew louder as I approached this certain area. The sound seemed to start with two beats, then stop and start all over again. Next, I heard what sounded like streams of water flowing followed by fierce winds moving in several different directions. At this time, I approached the bottom of a cliff where it was so bright at the top. I hadn't seen anything like any of the events I had been witnessing before, and this sight almost made me want to go back. But as I looked over the edge, a force of wind grabbed me and took me towards a bright light that seemed gentle, peaceful and warm.

I also remember looking back to the sound of voices. All I saw were little bright lights following me that got bigger as they came closer. Then I and these other bright lights, came out to an opening that was so overwhelming with loud sounds that were pleasant to hear. We just circled what appeared to be someone's big head. I looked down and saw a neck followed by shoulders with arms, a torso and legs which were sitting on a big chair. That was my vision and the revelation from it meant that I was a soul inside the body of God who had a host of other souls all following me. They must have been behind me the whole time. Some who have this same gift as I, are for the most part, more in tuned with the Holy Spirit and have more experience than I do.

These people are Seasoned True Believers in Christ Jesus, Prophets and Prophetess that follow the Word of God and listen carefully to His voice, but there are some who have this same gift and pervert it to make money. My Pastor from a long time ago said that, "Psychics are just Prophets and Prophetess that have missed their calling!" Without sounding like certain ones who have been to either place, I've written this by memory from all my dreams, visions and revelations that I've had over the years. Not to mention my own views with concerns followed by my own opinions and life journeys as well. For more of an understanding, I always look to the Word of God and undergo research for the truth!

Mostly, the main purpose of this writing is to open your heart and mind to Christ, which is, if you already haven't. I've spent years trying to perfect this writing, so I can send it out to someone it may help! After many rough drafts, adding something I forgot to add, then taking out what I felt didn't need to be in there, losing this writing and finding it again, I now feel it is ready to be read and re-read by anyone who has an ear for the truth. These revelations that I've written about is not to be taken lightly but to also learn from it!

Please don't take what I have written as fact, but read the Word of God for yourself. Seek through the scriptures in the Bible in backing every word you read in this book! I pray that this literature will help give you some insight about your own wellbeing! It is important to know that God operates within His own divine wisdom. Whenever He gives you a dream or vision, He will also give you the revelation from it. Your dream or vision may not meet the expectations of what anyone on earth that claims to be an expert about this subject or any given doctrines by degree holders as fact or truth. Sometimes, whatever God gives you may only be for you or for someone else. The Wisdom of God overrules anything that comes from Hell or Man, so lean not to your own understanding but the Wisdom of God our Father.

It is so important to understand that in getting an interpretation from a prophetic dream or vision, you need to acquire the skill from God our Father, so that you will know how to do this instead of relying on someone else to give it to you. I believe there are three ways to interpret your dream or vision. One of these three ways is the correct way. You can interpret with it coming from yourself, the Enemy or God our Father. Getting the skill from God is the correct way, not the other two and definitely not from psychics! You will open yourself up to demon activity if you visit a psychic for any reason!

If you are reading this and you are an Unbeliever, then please have an open mind to the things of God. Don't ever mock the Holy Spirit, because by grieving the Holy Spirit you cause damnation to come upon yourself! The events in this reading are meant to wake up those who are asleep in Christ, open the ears of the deaf and take off the blinders of those who choose folly over wisdom, so that they can see and hear the Word of God.

Do your own research to find out if what I am saying is true. I don't want anyone to go to Hell! For those that look for Christ, good for you. For those that are looking for something to fill the void in your lives...try Jesus! It's not hard to trust in a God that never fails, God never fails! Find yourself a spirit filled Church that you will grow in and follow the teachings of Jesus, stay in prayer, learn to worship and your faith will grow. Then, you'll please God! My own life experiences are that, Life Experiences.

My first reoccurring Prophetic Dream happened when I was 15 years old. God gave me the Revelation from it three years later. From these actions, I came to the realization that in everything, I was being shown and taught by God the Father. I'm still growing and learning from them. I'm 46 years old, and I feel like I have just barely scratched the surface!

Clean Heart

City Harvest Church – Lengki

"A clean heart, that's what I long for…

a heart that follows hard after thee

A clean heart, that's what I long for…

a heart that follows hard after thee

A heart that hides your word, so that

sin cannot come in…

A heart that's undivided, of one you

rule and reign…

A heart that beats compassion, that

Pleases you, my Lord, a sweet aroma of worship,

that rises to your Throne…

A clean heart…"

CHAPTER TWO

HEAVEN

Genesis 28:17 (ESV)

"And he was afraid and said, "How awesome is this place! This is none other than the house of God, and this is the gate of Heaven."

I was in my room staring at my reflection in the mirror and wondering if my life could ever get any better, because whatever I was doing wasn't working at all. As I sat on my bed feeling sorry for myself, I fell backwards, closed my eyes and started praying for God to do something in me. It felt like life had smacked me hard in the face then continued to laugh at my calamity. Then, I remember feeling so relaxed. When I opened my eyes and sat up, I looked around with shock; "This wasn't my room!" To my amazement, recognition set in, I was in HEAVEN!

This place was huge, bigger than life and almost 3-D looking. These thoughts as well as others all flooded my brain to an overwhelming sense of dizziness. There was a familiarity of this area. Then suddenly, I had an intense feeling of jubilation followed by an irresistible fascination of felicity in this enchanting harbor filled with a lasting abode of God. I was Home! Heaven is where we actually live. Earth is just a training ground for when we come back home. Some people, whether believers or not, can't grasp this accurate concept of fact. I wasn't dead or translated. I just figured that this was a dream, but it felt so real. The warmth I felt was not just from the outside but from within myself. I felt safe and my vision along with mind had more clarity and wisdom than before.

Philippians 3:20 (ESV)
".... But our citizenship is in heaven, and from it we await a Savior, the Lord Jesus Christ...."

As I walked around, I noticed the greenery all around me and the trees along with the grass and plants almost as if they were all smiling at me. This is just a simple normality because in heaven the most awesome is humble. Being in heaven was beyond belief. I had the uncanny ability to fly, so naturally I wanted to check out the sights. For what I was seeing, this was just too unreal, but there I was. I flew over to this field with tall emerald like green grass. The flowers were next of something magnificent which looked like they were paying attention to my every movement. Next, I came upon a stream of running water. As I followed it to see where it began or how far it went, there was a loud sound of water everywhere. A waterfall so big it made Niagara

Falls look puny. This waterfall fell into a lake of considerable size with land on each side. As I kept on looking, the land disappeared, and this lake seemed to run into what looked like an ocean.

Then, I flew through a wilderness passing up trees that literally waved at me as I went by. I couldn't tell what time it was or even know just how long I had spent up here so far. I finally stopped after all that sightseeing only to fall into a stare of the most beautiful picture with snowy mountain tops as a background of this monstrous city that appeared to have no end in sight. There were people and animals in the distance interacting with one another. Then I flew toward what looked like a courtyard. Just being here left me speechless. There were huge buildings with angels flying in and out of them, with a purpose I might add. The influence of these walls alone matched the feeling of strength and wisdom. There were also grape vines growing alongside of these walls which added a sense of classical elegance. I wasn't yet in the heart of Heaven where the great city resides, but there was so much to see just where I was at.

There were no signs of shadow anywhere. Everywhere I looked, light shined, and peace reigned. I wondered on for a bit when I came to some corridors. They seem to run on forever like a maze with doors on each side. Every door that I passed felt like some sort of knowledge in there for the taking. The power emulating from each door in passing was so intense.

I finally decided to go through one of these doors just to see what was on the other side, and to my amazement this room I had entered was almost bigger than I could comprehend! I was astounded to find out that this room was the ammunition that fueled all my questions and rejoined every one of the answers we often search for. There weren't any books or furniture nor signs of life, but in this room was a power unlike anything I've ever imagined but with a feeling of immense worship and meditation. As a human, it is very difficult to record or measure time in any fashion up here. If memory serves me correctly, a thousand years on earth is equal to one day in Heaven. Every time I think on this, it transcends into abstract thought.

2 Peter 3:8 (ESV)
"But do not overlook this one fact, beloved, that with the Lord one day is as a thousand years, and a thousand years as one day."

    Heaven is a vast universe of infinite possibilities that has the power to produce effects in the heart and mind, Heaven also infiltrates the inner man empowering the Holy Spirit within.

    Meanwhile, walking down these corridors after leaving that room, I noticed that all the walkways were paved with diamonds, pearls and some sort of crystal. As I turned the corner, I was staring at a golden street. On one side of this priceless jewel of pavement was a series of mansions, and on the other side was an enormous body of water that was as beautiful and as clear as crystal. Then out of nowhere, this thought came to me. 'This body of water is called the Sea of Forgiveness which both mansion and sea would only be for the overcomers.' I pondered a few questions for a while. Why that name? If I were to swim in this body of water, will I be forgiven or is this just for the ones that have already been forgiven?

    My mind was racing to make sense of it all, and these questions could've been coming from me. In other words, I was brainstorming questions and trying to make sense of all of it. I was also still learning as a young Christian. Then like a bolt of lightning, this statement hit me, "If you're in Heaven, then that means you are an OverComer!" My dream seemed to be jumbled around, but I was in the right ballpark.

John 14:2&3 (KJV)
"In my Father's house are many mansions: if it were not so, I would have told you. I go to prepare a place for you. And if I go and prepare a place for you, I will come again, and receive you unto myself; that where I am, there ye may be also."

Acts 17:24 (KJV)
"God that made the world and all things therein, seeing that he is Lord of heaven and earth, dwelleth not in temples made with hands...."

Isaiah 66:1 (KJV)
"Thus, saith the LORD, the heaven is my throne, and the earth is my footstool: where is the house that ye build unto me? And where is the place of my rest?"

Psalms 132:13&14 (KJV)
"For the LORD hath chosen Zion; he hath desired it for his habitation. This is my rest for ever: here will I dwell; for I have desired it."

"We are Zion because the Lord God has made it that way and God dwells within each one of us! When Jesus said that there where many mansions to be prepared for us, His words were parabolic, not literally meaning mansions but rooms for us in His Fathers' house".

John 14:23 (KJV)
"Jesus answered and said unto him, if a man love me, he will keep my words: and my Father will love him, and we will come unto him, and make our abode with him."

1 Corinthians 3:16 (KJV)
"Know ye not that ye are the temple of God, and that the Spirit of God dwelleth in you?"

Where do your sins go after God has forgiven you? Your sins go into the Sea of God's Forgetfulness, never to be remembered again. There is no unforgiveness in Heaven.

Micah 7:18&19 (ESV)
"Who is a God like you, pardoning iniquity and passing over transgression for the remnant of his inheritance? He does not retain his anger forever, because he delights in steadfast love. He will again have compassion on us; he will tread our iniquities underfoot. You will cast all our sins into the depths of the sea."

1 Corinthians 2:12-14 (ESV)
"Now we have received not the spirit of the world, but the Spirit who is from God, that we might understand the things freely given us by God. And we impart this in words not taught by human wisdom but taught by the Spirit, interpreting spiritual truths to those who are spiritual. The natural person does not accept the things of the Spirit of God, for they are folly to him, and he is not able to understand them because they are spiritually discerned."

Revelation 4:6 (ESV)
"....and before the throne there was as it were a sea of glass, like crystal. And around the throne, on each side of the throne, are four living creatures, full of eyes in front and behind...."

You've got to love the human mind. The dreams we have to the best of our ability shows us just how far we've come whether believer or not. I believe that God showed me Heaven in a way that I could grasp, because He knows my tenacity for learning His Perfect Word! **The sight of both mansion and sea was magnificently matched by its magnitude of imperialism and an historic inheritance of pure elegance.**

I wondered just how big Heaven really was, so I flew up to a distance what could have been like hundreds of thousands of feet up in the air. When I stopped, I looked down and to my surprise I was looking at Heaven in the shape of a man! The entire kingdom has gates around it, just like the Great Wall of China. The Kingdom of Heaven is so big and the great city itself is sitting on a big hill. The kingdom is literally an outline of a body. Although the throne room is where the heart is located, the busiest part is at the head and the entrance is at the feet. I was reminded of a fort or one of those big kingdoms like the ones in medieval times, but in this kingdom many castles and mansions stay. The main castle where the throne room resides is surrounded by powerful looking angels!

Heaven is as big as a planet or bigger. Now, when I had this revelation so many years ago, I was still learning about the Spirit Realm, Heaven, Hell and everything that complements them, so I might have been just a little bit off but still within these parameters.

1 Corinthians 2:9 (ESV)
"But, as it is written, "What no eye has seen, nor ear heard, nor the heart of man imagined, what God has prepared for those who love him"

Still looking down, I focused upon the ankle area and at the sole of the foot was this area of darkness. Almost frightening, I couldn't tell what it was, but it looked like an abyss. This area that changed from many different shades of black and gray, but with a rotating color that faded in and out. The mere sight of this was in fact frightening, but I was unafraid. This just reminded me of an Evangelist, who was a guest speaker that came to my church some time ago and shared his testimony with the congregation of which in his testimony he said similar to this same displacement. This is the same Evangelist whose nickname used be Satan. This was also the same Evangelist who back in the day was one of the three founders of a major gang that started in Sunday School was used by God in such a way by bringing others to the Kingdom of God. Last I heard, these gangs show him respect and let him come to share just what the Lord God has done for him!

I marveled at the fact that there was even a place this dark up here, but I also remembered Judgment Day isn't all that pleasant either! I remember a strange report about the Black Hole. I learned of three reports while attending a certain sprit filled church. The first report was about the Black Hole. Two astronauts inside their space shuttle on a mission totally discovered it by accident. In the middle of this vast darkness was a shimmer or a hole with light coming through. For a split second, there was movement that really caught both the astronauts' eyes. They tried to see more with their telescope, but nothing was seen, so they reported these findings to Headquarters. This was explained in Church as a fact that really happened, but I'm sure it has been denied and I can't find any references or any more information on this subject. This was told and explained in Church many years ago, so these details could be off, but I cannot find the original report. There are pictures from the Hubble Telescope taken in space, check them out.

The second report was about a few scientists in Siberia that drilled deep down into the earth only to hear torturing sounds as if people were down in the earth's core being tortured. All this was heard with their listening devices. There were some that mentioned about what happened in Siberia, but the reports are somewhat different then what I learned in church back then. The third report was about the late Jacque Cousteau where on his last adventure under water in which he heard the same sounds as the scientists did, but these sounds were coming from beneath the ocean floor which was around the Bermuda Triangle. These sounds were described as whips, chains, laughter, yells and screams.

Jacque Cousteau passed away shortly after that, and his legacy was continued on by his son. All three reports may not be proven true only because after each event happened, the information was kept quiet except for a few leaks here and there. I could be wrong in my assumption, at least that's what some would say, if they would polish off their blinders. I did some more digging and found more info on the late Jacque Cousteau. He was swimming over in the Sea of Cuba, and that's where he heard the screams and torture sounds. One of Cousteau's staff heard the same thing I might add. The sounds of Hell from Siberia were analyzed, and there was some ancient Arabic language coming from the recording.

There are many wonders that can't be counted or recorded in space, and most of what goes on in space is too complex to understand. So, maybe that's why theories and educated guesses are formed. Didn't scientist say that we evolved from Apes and called it a fact? Later, these same scientists tried to prove Christ as a farce and proved that Humans were created and started from Eve by accident. There was this Billionaire that was a genius who said that, "There was no God," and what he said was challenged and defeated by a child. The spirit of confusion is running wild in this World, so that is why we must stay close to our God of Wisdom and Peace.

Isaiah 19:14, 45:16 (ESV)
"The LORD has mingled within her a spirit of confusion, and they will make Egypt stagger in all its deeds, as a drunken man staggers in his vomit."

"All of them are put to shame and confounded; the makers of idols go in confusion together."

Acts 19:32 (ESV)
"Now some cried out one thing, some another, for the assembly was in confusion, and most of them did not know why they had come together."

1 Corinthians 14:33 (ESV)
"For God is not a God of confusion but of peace. As in all the churches of the saints...."

I touched back down from my verticality and started walking around. There were many people while in passing. Because I was in Heaven, I wanted so badly just to run into someone from the past. I'd look at the people in passing and think, 'What if I met King David, what I could say to a man of so much fame and humility? What about Samson, who in my opinion could've been six foot three or taller? I'd guess him to weigh over two hundred and fifty pounds, even though some believe he was an average size man.' Questions flooded my mind about Samson's strength and Wisdom, realizing that his strength was a legendary sanction that could only come from Yahweh, Father of all creation!

Judges 14:5 & 6, 15:14-17 (ESV)
"Then Samson went down with his father and mother to Timnah, and they came to the vineyards of Timnah. And behold, a young lion came toward him roaring. Then the Spirit of the LORD rushed upon him, and although he had nothing in his hand, he tore the lion in pieces as one tears a young goat. But he did not tell his father or his mother what he had done."

"When he came to Lehi, the Philistines came shouting to meet him. Then the Spirit of the LORD rushed upon him, and the ropes that were on his arms became as flax that has caught fire, and his bonds melted off his hands. And he found a fresh jawbone of a donkey, and put out his hand and took it, and with it he struck 1,000 men. And Samson said, "With the jawbone of a donkey, heaps upon heaps, with the jawbone of a donkey have I struck down a thousand men."

As soon as he had finished speaking, he threw away the jawbone out of his hand. And that place was called Ramath-lehi."

There were many acts of great leadership, strength and wisdom followed by an insightful arrogance and failure that was recorded and talked about that he did back on earth before returning to Heaven but before all the greatness and his position of power that came to be, Samson had to be right for the Lord to use him...even in the event of his death! This is what I mean, spending time with the Father even when you don't think you've got that kind of time, make time because your true test of time will begin when you know the truth so taking by force what Satan has stolen from you is a very good start! Prayer and fasting followed by countless hours in the presence of the Holy Spirit, we must start somewhere right?

Even though God had many people with different testimonies, why do you think God used Samson for a testimony so great? I came to this conclusion, In the past where the atmosphere was cleaner, men had exceptional strength and so with Samson's strength through God must have been a holy type of strength that no man could measure whether it be fantasy or real life. Well, there are different reasons that aren't listed below, but I tend to lean on the reason of because Israel needed to be shook up! There were several different Judges before Samson that didn't have his strength but also judged with the approval of God. With what Samson's strength was about must have also been the same type of strength David had when slew the lion, the bear and Goliath!

1 Samuel 17:36 & 37 (ESV)

"Your servant has struck down both lions and bears, and this uncircumcised Philistine shall be like one of them, for he has defied the armies of the living God." And David said, "The LORD who delivered me from the paw of the lion and from the paw of the bear will deliver me from the hand of this Philistine." And Saul said to David, "Go, and the LORD be with you!"

First, David doesn't go into battle with any hesitation, calculation or question of fear, but he is expecting the result to be in his favor and his confidence in God was in full effect. **"Let no man's heart fail him. Your servant will fight with this uncircumcised Philistine."** We can all learn from this, with the highest of results. Not every Man can relate to Samson, but they can surely relate to David. I kept fantasizing about who I could meet when Job just popped into my head. I'll bet he was a very unusually regimented type of man with the perfect retrospection on Gods' love and promises.

Job 1:1 (ESV)
"There was a man in the land of Uz whose name was Job, and that man was blameless and upright, one who feared God and turned away from evil."

I continued to take in more sights as I noticed all the people had an individual glow, and the Angels all waved as they flew by. I thought to myself, 'How beautiful…I'm in Heaven, I'm back Home!' I stood with my head held high and a smile that ran for miles. I would always daydream about all kinds of things and events ever since I was little. I found myself smack in the middle of an amazing courtyard and surprisingly enough. I was pleasantly approached by seven white horses without a single blemish, then all these horses went to one knee as if they were bowing to me. I was simply dumbfounded, so I bowed back.

On earth, I've never seen or heard of a horse bow all the way to the ground, let alone to one knee. I didn't think this was possible, but all things are possible in Heaven. This was a rare treat. In the Circus, they can train a horse to do that, but this was different, REAL DIFFERENT!

Behind me came a much-distilled voice that said that I was indeed a special young man to have seven horses bow at the same time in a profound respect only for me at that time. Also adding that these horses only gather together for something special.

I turned around to a man from the past. A Native American with such a deep sense of wisdom, peace and an understanding of God was so overwhelming that it just knocked me off my feet! Then, it hit me like a ton of bricks! There are many nationalities in Heaven not just black or white. There is only one race and this race has more than one color, Humanity! I don't know exactly why I assumed that there were only two or three nationalities in Heaven. Maybe it's because of what some of us learn in Church or Sunday School. Maybe it's just me not paying attention in class or service. As the moment passed, I realized that everything in Heaven revolved around God!

I had the most unforgettable conversation with this man who spoke with so much knowledge and wisdom. He never revealed to me what Tribe he was from or his age, but he looked about over a hundred years old or more and his demeanor was young. His name was Hero-Black Feather. We spoke for some time on his past life as he lived on earth. While he spoke, I was simply astounded just to hear what it was really like back then. Hero explained to me how everything was so much purer than it is today. The food was healthier with no added chemicals, and the sky was clearer than today with no threat of ozone!

People lived longer back in those days which meant that everything was healthier with no pollution at all. Plus, people in general were more in tuned with God, not like now where today's society is trying to turn the precious name of God into a generic name! There are more sacrilegious ways today than there were yesterday, and the temptations seem to have grown a great deal. Heaven is made up of cities full of people, mountains where eagles reside, fields of wilderness teaming with wildlife, rivers of life overflowing, oceans that are filled with many different underwater creatures and angels everywhere you turn. Wherever I went, I heard in song, "Glory to God in the Highest!"

Revelation 5:8-14, 19:1-7 (ESV)

"And when he had taken the scroll, the four living creatures and the twenty-four elders fell down before the Lamb, each holding a harp, and golden bowls full of incense, which are the prayers of the saints.

And they sang a new song, saying, "Worthy are you to take the scroll and to open its seals, for you were slain, and by your blood you ransomed people for God from every tribe and language and people and nation, and you have made them a kingdom and priests to our God, and they shall reign on the earth."

Then I looked, and I heard around the throne and the living creatures and the elders the voice of many angels, numbering myriads of myriads and thousands of thousands, saying with a loud voice, "Worthy is the Lamb who was slain, to receive power and wealth and wisdom and might and honor and glory and blessing!" And I heard every creature in heaven and on earth and under the earth and in the sea, and all that is in them, saying, "To him who sits on the throne and to the Lamb be blessing and honor and glory and might forever and ever!" And the four living creatures said, "Amen!" and the elders fell down and worshiped."

"After this I heard what seemed to be the loud voice of a great multitude in heaven, crying out, "Hallelujah! Salvation and glory and power belong to our God, for his judgments are true and just; for he has judged the great prostitute who corrupted the earth with her immorality and has avenged on her the blood of his servants."

Once more they cried out, "Hallelujah! The smoke from her goes up forever and ever." And the twenty-four elders and the four living creatures fell down and worshiped God who was seated on the throne, saying, "Amen. Hallelujah!"

And from the throne came a voice saying, "Praise our God, all you his servants, you who fear him, small and great."

And a voice came from the throne, saying, "Give praise to our God, all you His bond-servants, you who fear Him, the small and the great." Then I heard something like the voice of a great multitude and like the sound of many waters and like the sound of mighty peals of thunder, saying, "Hallelujah! For the Lord our God, the Almighty, reigns.

"Let us rejoice and be glad and give the glory to Him, for the marriage of the Lamb has come and His bride has made herself ready."

I thought I'd seen everything and looked in every corner. But every time I turned around, there was a new area of Heaven that I somehow missed, almost as if either hiding or just built. I had the impression of Heaven as a huge maze that went on forever and that searching Heaven is like "A needle in a haystack." In other words, you'd never be able to uncover more than half of it. In the beginning, when God made the heavens and the earth, the cosmos went haywire and it has never been the same. In our very existence, we are only specks in this great universe ruled by the Father God Almighty!

After speaking with Hero for a time, I sat down in a field after walking a great distance and took in as much as I only could. I was paralyzed with a resounding stalemate where everything was enhanced almost like reality just shifted to a different plain of existence. Then it hit me again...I was in another dimension! There are three Heavens that exist. The first Heaven is above our heads, but underneath the stars where our planes and helicopters fly. The second Heaven is space, where the stars and planets are; not to mention that this is also where the Devil and his demons' dwell. The third Heaven is where no one knows. I believe it is either on the other side of the Black Hole or in another dimension; maybe they're both right.

I remembered back in bible study, one of the topics we were studying on was about lawyers. In this study, we focused on Jesus as our lawyer while Satan was our accuser. With that being said, an Angel came over and led me to a city.

1 John 2:1-3 (ESV)

"My little children, I am writing these things to you so that you may not sin. But if anyone does sin, we have an advocate with the Father, Jesus Christ the righteous. He is the propitiation for our sins, and not for ours only but also for the sins of the whole world. And by this we know that we have come to know him, if we keep his commandments."

As we went through a series of corridors, we came to a stop and right in front of me was this door of such a craftsmanship so beautifully filled with an artwork that was truly amazing.

Then the angel opened the door to this room that was fantastically unimaginable but very well distinguished with stained glass windows which spoke of the Fathers' everlasting glory. I had to pinch myself every few minutes just because of this new reality. When I entered this room, I was totally speechless. I was in an actual court room but on a Heavenly level. We were up in the balconies, and down below us was were tribunals raged on. This was truly an extraordinary but unique type situation.

Matthew 5:25 (ESV)

"Come to terms quickly with your accuser while you are going with him to court, lest your accuser hand you over to the judge, and the judge to the guard, and you be put in prison."

2 Chronicles 19:4-11 (ESV)

"Jehoshaphat lived at Jerusalem. And he went out again among the people, from Beersheba to the hill country of Ephraim, and brought them back to the LORD, the God of their fathers. He appointed judges in the land in all the fortified cities of Judah, city by city, and said to the judges, "Consider what you do, for you judge not for man but for the LORD. He is with you in giving judgment.

Now then, let the fear of the LORD be upon you. Be careful what you do, for there is no injustice with the LORD our God, or partiality or taking bribes." Moreover, in Jerusalem Jehoshaphat appointed certain Levites and priests and heads of families of Israel, to give judgment for the LORD and to decide disputed cases. They had their seat at Jerusalem.

And he charged them: "Thus you shall do in the fear of the LORD, in faithfulness, and with your whole heart: whenever a case comes to you from your brothers who live in their cities, concerning bloodshed, law or commandment, statutes or rules, then you shall warn them, that they may not incur guilt before the LORD and wrath may not come upon you and your brothers.

Thus, you shall do, and you will not incur guilt. And behold, Amariah the chief priest is over you in all matters of the LORD; and Zebadiah the son of Ishmael, the governor of the house of Judah,

in all the king's matters, and the Levites will serve you as officers. Deal courageously, and may the LORD be with the upright!"

In the bible study, I remembered someone saying first that God the Father allows Satan to do whatever but with restrictions and not to cross over any certain boundaries. The second thing was that in a man's' prayers, no demon in hell could touch him or his family if they had the Blood of Christ on them. But if the door to sin is opened, all bets are off! It's nice to know that even in our folly, we're never perfect but perfectly forgiven.

Luke 10:17 (ESV)
The seventy-two returned with joy, saying, "Lord, even the demons are subject to us in your name!"

Psalms 19:9 (ESV)
".... the fear of the LORD is clean, enduring forever; the rules of the LORD are true, and righteous altogether."

Psalms 103:19 (ESV)
"The LORD has established his throne in the heavens, and his kingdom rules over all."

There are always rules that are laid down for Satan and his minions to follow. The beauty in this is that they've got no choice in the matter, and they must follow whatever rules that is set before them. If there is something meant for evil, God turns it into good! I pondered why God would even allow Satan to do anything let alone give him a boundary not to cross. But suddenly, I remembered that free will was given to everyone from the Father, and that there was a way out of temptation through the Blood of the Lamb. Also, the fact being is that God uses Satan in some situations for our benefit, so we can learn!

It is true that the Father does give even His mighty Angels Free Will, a gift that all of His Creation has; even Satan. The Fallen Angels that were spoken about in Genesis, Jude and Revelation concerning how they fell by losing their position; they had Free Will as well. Then

I woke up, not from a deep sleep, but from a vision which felt so real. In my teens is when I started having these dreams, visions and revelations. I had the most unforgettable dreams about Hell and being left behind. It scared me so bad that I never forgot how it felt, and these dreams were the first of many visions, dreams and strong revelations!

Caught in a phantom of actuality, this illusion is a startling reality from the beginning as an inauguration of consummation. This didn't feel like the end. It felt more like an opening to a new era where time has no meaning, and I was in for the ride of my life!

At a very young age, I made the decision to have an open mind about lots of things but mostly when it came to the spirit realm. I've seen many things that would send chills up and down your spine. One day, I prayed and told God that I wanted to understand the spirit realm to know what's really going on. But when it came to demons, that's where I drew the line so that's why I see things through the sprit. Sometimes, I hear things that are disturbing only to later find out something wicked just took place! As I grow in my Faith Walk, I collect any and all information that comes to me from God our Father. I Love the Word of God, and I want to learn as much as I can...or as much as God will allow. God my Father is preparing me for something, but I haven't a clue what it is. When I'm ready for whatever He has for me to do and wants me to see or hear, I will be ready!

For His Glory

For His glory I was born;
As I swim across the sea of tranquility
And I glide on the wings of love
I can feel His holy presence with sincerity
As I fly through the air like a dove...
For His glory I was born;
And into this world I came
To learn and spread the gospel of Gods' holy light
To sing His holy praises for all, one and the same
And to engage into this spiritual fight...
For His glory I was born;
I can almost taste the fruit of the Holy Spirit
I can almost feel the face of the Living God
I can almost see the kingdom as I flow near it
I can almost smell a fragrance long and broad...
For His glory I was born;
As Yahweh looks down on me with His great approval
And I know He'll always be there with me
And be it known to all Men, I shall always be favorable
Because Adonai shows me how to see...
For His glory I was born;
To praise and worship in His holy temple
To teach the truth and to love as high as the highest star
To preach to the unreachable and make His word simple
To enter the holy battle and with a loud sound, blow the Shofar...
For His glory I was born;
As a solider I stand strong just like the oak tree
With battle scars and a prize to win
This fight has already been won, we've beaten sin
Because now I've got the victory!
For His glory I was born;

Matthew 7:21-23 (ESV)
"Not everyone who says to me, 'Lord, Lord,' will enter the kingdom of heaven, but the one who does the will of my Father who is in heaven. On that day many will say to me, 'Lord, Lord, did we not prophesy in your name, and cast out demons in your name, and do many mighty works in your name? And then will I declare to them, 'I never knew you; depart from me, you workers of lawlessness."

CHAPTER THREE

HELL

2 PETER 2:4 (ESV)

"For if God did not spare angels when they sinned, but cast them into Hell and committed them to chains of gloomy darkness to be kept until the judgment..."

Once again, I started to have another vision. This time it felt different, almost like I was seeing this take place as it happened! Facing the gates, I turned around to a paradox, a vast blackness with the likeness of an abyss and at that very moment I took a step back. Jesus was standing just a few yards in front of me. Also, in front of him stood nine people, all who were waiting to enter the gates of Heaven. They all looked nervous and for a good reason I might add! Hell......what is it like? For the Overcomer, they will never know. For the Nonbeliever, the Backslider, the Rejecter of Christ and anyone that has the mark of the World still on them, they shall know endless pain and great turmoil in ways that cannot be explained or expressed!

Hell has been joked upon for a long time, but those that joked about it, didn't even realize that Hell was or is knocking on their door. Hell has places, areas, events, departments, monsters and demons which exist just for those unfortunate souls that come there. Everything in Hell is more demonic, has more chaos, has unlimited torture that is so unbearable and so unbelievable to even comprehend. Hell is Evil!

Amazingly enough, everyone I looked at I somehow knew. I wondered how this could be possible and then it hit me like a ton of bricks, in the light, darkness cannot hide! All these people were to receive their sentence. Derek was a back slider, which three days before his sudden death he finally sold out to Christ. Jake was just saved on his death bed. Simon died in prison with a life sentence without the possibility of parole. He was never bitter and still asked for forgiveness. Then he led two inmates and four prison guards to Christ!

Tim was killed by a bear, but to my relief he didn't suffer and was a born-again Christian. This brother had no common sense at all!

Karen died defending three young children over in Cuba on a mission trip, and because of her actions the children were all saved! Jesus looked at everyone that was just now mentioned and said; "Well-done thou good and faithful servants enter into joy today!" One by one they entered the gates of Heaven. I realized that seeing these peoples' past was amazing, because everything the person did was brought to the light whether good or bad. It was like a gigantic movie screen that showed each ones' history.

Hebrews 11:13 (ESV)

"These all died in faith, not having received the things promised, but having seen them and greeted them from afar, and having acknowledged that they were strangers and exiles on the earth."

After Karen, this left one man and three women. Denny lived the life of a fool and was eventually turned over to a reprobate mind. Margaret participated in orgies, then after sleeping through an alter call, she later was struck by a speeding car and died instantly. Julie killed her unborn by means of abortion which during her last procedure died on the operating table from internal bleeding. Rebecca became a Witch through the Satanist Church and later died willingly for a sacrifice. All who were left received their final sentence.

Just then, Jesus spoke those dreadful words that no one in their right mind wanted to hear. These words cut right through me as He said, "I know thee not thou doers' of iniquity, depart from me ye cursed into outer darkness and spend an eternity weeping and gnashing of the teeth in everlasting fire prepared for the devil and his angels!" As those dreadful words left His mouth, it felt like my soul sank just a little deeper. Then suddenly like a magnet I was being pulled forward as the four people took off toward this paradox screaming at the top of their lungs as if all sanity had left them behind and as they reached the edge, just like baby squirrels with no fear; their plunge was a swift one.

Hebrews 10:26 (ESV)

"For if we go on sinning deliberately after receiving the knowledge of the truth, there no longer remains a sacrifice for sins...."

By this time, I was a hysterical mess. Then Jesus appeared to me and said, "Peace be Still." So, even though I was falling towards what looked like a bunch of huge worms coming out from a big ball of fire with their mouths wide open surrounded by four screaming people that sounded like a school of banshee in the utmost inscrutable pain, and not to mention I was on my way to Hell...I was calm. While in descent to my destination, I looked up hoping to catch just a glimpse of my savior, but Heaven had passed out of sight!

Then, I focused onto where I was headed, and to my surprise my eyes were fixed on Hell but in the shape of a man just like Heaven, but in such a deformed fashion by way of counterfeit or imitation.

Matthew 10:28 (ESV)

"And do not fear those who kill the body but cannot kill the soul. Rather fear him who can destroy both soul and body in hell."

When we finally touched down, these heinously hideous creatures came from out of nowhere and grabbed Denny and Julie before they had a chance to even stand on their own two feet. The most startling was Rebecca. She landed on her feet with almost no effort at all and began walking away without any fear of demons trying to grab her. Rebecca walked over to a throne made in honor just for her with demons surrounding and bowing in respect. The way she acted was almost as though she thought Hell would do her bidding. As she sat in this seat made for royalty, this so-called throne clamped her down where she couldn't move voluntarily. An unforeseen force caused her to jerk hard back and forth and side to side violently. She started screaming as her flesh rotted off while these same demons walked around her chanting the same incantations, she used on the surface several times before which in turn made her soul turn dim in the most painful way imaginable.

For those that are confused with me saying, "On the surface" and not "in Hell," you must by now realize that Hell is literally under our feet, either near it or in the earths' core! While this was going on, Margaret who was already running for her life knew better, because she knew just what would happen to her for an eternity if she were caught. For the Christians that know the truth and what is really going on, if they go to Hell, it is much worse for them because they back slid and wasn't sincere in their hearts for forgiveness. They know better because they Know the Truth! Jesus can't save you if you reject His Salvation!

These hideous demons were laughing so hysterically. The mere sound ripped right through me. It was a horrifying dreadful type of laughter which I had never in my life encountered...it was an Evil sound! Margaret tried to run to safety but ran right into the arms of one of the demons. Then three more came out from the shadows and were all laughing. She begged them to kill her, but they all mocked her as the demon that grabbed her released his hold and said, "You're free to go."

She turned and tried to run, but an invisible force jerked her backwards and then brought her to her knees. She then started to do what she used to do when she was still alive. She was going to be doing this in Hell for an eternity! I was floored because she had no control over her actions. I tried to turn my head, but I couldn't. I had no control over just turning my head and I couldn't even close my own eyes, so I saw and heard everything which made me sick to my stomach! Having no control over my own body really scared me, but this also let me know that this is one of the ways of torture in Hell! I looked over to the left of the orgy and witnessed an extensive line of demons. I was in disbelief and those demons just had their way with her.

Finally, I was able to move only to witness Denny being thrown into a reoccurring fiery pit, and Julie was carried off by one of the demons to relive the worst abortion she ever had. An abortion is genocide because when a fetus is aborted, you're killing not only the fetus but also the children of who would have been and that Bloodline is destroyed. It is wrong to murder a person. The unborn is a person, and therefore, it is wrong to murder the unborn! Being born means to come from the Mother's womb, and the unborn is still alive even though the unborn child is in the mother's body.

Deuteronomy 24:6 (ESV)
"No one shall take a mill or an upper millstone in pledge, for that would be taking a life in pledge."

I had a selfish moment with a sigh of relief that these demons couldn't see me; although, with some of them looking in my direction, sometimes I wondered. This was not the Hell I had learned about when I was in Children's Church, and not very many sermons that are preached explain the evil of Hell. This place had more evil and perversity than anything I ever imagined, but the torture was so unreal. This Hell was so intensely antagonistic which made it the worst evil around the globe look like child's play!

Our Father gives us many chances to make our life right by the repentance of our sins. Jesus shed His perfect blood for us so that we could be saved, but many people aren't taking this act of grace and forgiveness seriously. The sad part about this is that most of the people that aren't taking their salvation seriously are Christians, and ALL Christians know the truth but most of them think like a child with manipulation in their hearts. They act as though they can sin, and God will forgive them no matter how many times they sin. You can't sin without remorse to receive forgiveness, can't work like that!

Romans 1:28 (ESV)

"And since they did not see fit to acknowledge God, God gave them up to a debased mind to do what ought not to be done."

I wondered over to some ruins where there in the middle was a fire pit, but right next to it was an oil pit. I thought to myself, 'What kind of evil are they planning now?' Then low and behold more demons showed up with more people to torture. These people looked like a native tribe with strange markings on their bodies. The demons dipped everyone who was in that tribe inside the oil pit, one by one, and then they threw them into the fire and repeated this act without ceasing. I turned my head in horror and disbelief. It broke my heart seeing this, but there was a reason for all of this. This entire tribe back on the surface was so wicked that only three small innocent children were saved!

Romans 1:18-32 (ESV)

"For the wrath of God is revealed from heaven against all ungodliness and unrighteousness of men, who by their unrighteousness suppress the truth. For what can be known about God is plain to them, because God has shown it to them. For his invisible attributes, namely, his eternal power and divine nature, have been clearly perceived, ever since the creation of the world, in the things that have been made. So, they are without excuse.

For although they knew God, they did not honor him as God or give thanks to him, but they became futile in their thinking, and their foolish hearts were darkened. Claiming to be wise, they became fools, and exchanged the glory of the immortal God for images resembling mortal man and birds and animals and creeping things. Therefore, God gave them up in the lusts of their hearts to impurity, to the dishonoring of their bodies among themselves, because they exchanged the truth about God for a lie and worshiped and served the creature rather than the Creator, who is blessed forever!

Amen.

For this reason, God gave them up to dishonorable passions. For their women exchanged natural relations for those that are contrary to nature; and the men likewise gave up natural relations with women and were consumed with passion for one another, men committing shameless acts with men and receiving in themselves the due penalty for their error.

And since they did not see fit to acknowledge God, God gave them up to a debased mind to do what ought not to be done. They

were filled with all manner of unrighteousness, evil, covetousness, malice. They are full of envy, murder, strife, deceit, maliciousness. They are gossips, slanderers, haters of God, insolent, haughty, boastful, inventors of evil, disobedient to parents, foolish, faithless, heartless, ruthless. Though they know God's decree that those who practice such things deserve to die, they not only do them but give approval to those who practice them."

I moved on when I stopped dead in my tracks. Only in disbelief did I stand there dumb founded. I couldn't believe my eyes when this one demon came out of the shadows; Shrek! This demon had the likeness of Shrek. Not only did it sound like him, but it also walked like him. The Shrek looking thing was giving orders and the demons were all obeying. I had this Revelation of Hell way before the movie Shrek was even thought of, I might add! Now each demon had a specific look to it. They all had one thing in common that stood out from all the evil that each one had. One by one these demons all reminded me of all the horror flicks I used to either watch or have never seen, but just knew about.

It was almost as if someone spent time in Hell and captured some of the likeness from every demon they could find then put it wherever people could see it. Everything that I experienced up to this point was more graphic then anything I ever imagined, but I had a job to do, so I moved on. As I moved about freely, I saw and heard people being tortured and tormented everywhere.

There was this one guy who died from a hunting accident. Every few minutes these demons that looked like those Xenomorphs from the movie Alien would come at him with no mercy and rip him to shreds. After the torture was over, he would simultaneously piece right back together, and this odious action would repeat all over again. I was puzzled. What could he have done on earth to deserve such a punishment like this?

Genesis 9:6 (ESV)

"Whoever sheds the blood of man, by man shall his blood be shed, for God made man in his own image."

So, I guess whatever he did to someone was equal to this perverted and atrocious act. Next, I came over to a series of fire pits and in one of the pits was a teenager. I thought to myself, 'How could this be, this isn't for children? Some of these people just couldn't have done anything so despicable for this to be their own reward! Then Jesus came and said to me that different people have different sins. It does break His heart, but He won't go against free will even if it means that Hell could be their new home! Everyone does have a choice in the matter, but it's up to them if they want to listen.

The next thing that happened twisted my stomach into a knot. I was staring at two different homosexual couples. There were two gay men and two lesbian women being tortured in a way that I wish I could forget. There were demons all around them. Living in a Homosexual lifestyle is dangerous not only to your physical body but also to your spirit man, and whatever you do can affect the innocent as well. Whatever spirit that is not of God will be ultimately destroyed unless Jesus is allowed to intervene. The people who practice Homosexuality,

Pedophilia, Witchcraft and other wicked activities are against the Father God and will not inherit the Kingdom of Heaven. I've heard of people who claim to be 'Homosexual Christians,' and there is no such thing. This is confusion which comes from Satan.

Someone who claims to be a Homosexual Christian is picking, choosing and justifying whatever kind of lifestyle they want. They think that God the Father will accept them as a Homosexual Christian in Heaven because they are good Christians. The problem with that reasoning is that however you look at it, Homosexuality is a sin whether you are a Christian in your own mind or not. Homosexual and Christian are two different words with two different meanings which cannot be a part of each other. Like oil and water, these two don't mix!

These people are spending an eternity in Hell for becoming a part of what I sometimes call a Chaos of Abomination, many different reasons of why this is a destination for many different people from many different walks of life. The Word of God is just, and no one is above the Word of the God! Homosexuality has been around since after Adam. It's just out more and starting to become widely accepted in our present time, and the colors of the Rainbow isn't for Homosexual use. This is part of the reason why, these last days are called, 'The Days of Noah!'

Genesis 9:12-15 (ESV)

"And God said, "This is the sign of the covenant that I make between me and you and every living creature that is with you, for all future generations: I have set my bow in the cloud, and it shall be a sign of the covenant between me and the earth. When I bring clouds over the earth and the bow is seen in the clouds, I will remember my covenant that is between me and you and every living creature of all flesh. And the waters shall never again become a flood to destroy all flesh".

Romans 1:24-32 (ESV)

"Therefore, God gave them up in the lusts of their hearts to impurity, to the dishonoring of their bodies among themselves, because they exchanged the truth about God for a lie and worshiped and served the creature rather than the Creator, who is blessed forever! Amen. For this reason, God gave them up to dishonorable passions.

For their women exchanged natural relations for those that are contrary to nature; and the men likewise gave up natural relations with women and were consumed with passion for one another, men committing shameless acts with men and receiving in themselves the due penalty for their error. And since they did not see fit to acknowledge God, God gave them up to a debased mind to do what ought not to be done.

They were filled with all manner of unrighteousness, evil, covetousness, malice. They are full of envy, murder, strife, deceit, maliciousness. They are gossips, slanderers, haters of God, insolent, haughty, boastful, inventors of evil, disobedient to parents, foolish, faithless, heartless, ruthless. Though they know God's decree that those who practice such things deserve to die, they not only do them but give approval to those who practice them."

Then I heard a splashing sound, so I looked in the direction from where it was coming from. It occurred to me.... water down here? Again, I was dumbfounded. It was a huge Lake of Fire as far as my eye could see! After seeing that representation of pain everlasting, I moved on without as much as a thought. Every fire pit had one to three people in it. Some fire pits burned constantly while other fire pits burned every few minutes almost as if to give the victim a break from torment. This pit is a reoccurring fire pit...it is a vicious tease! When some of the people first arrive here, their bodies are intact. But over an abbreviated period of time, their flesh rots completely off while their souls' dim from a bright color to a black dirty color. In this process there is great pain!

Some get thrown into a fire pit were their flesh melts away and their souls burn constantly, unless you're one of the unlucky souls that gets a reoccurring fire pit as a home. These fire pits burn hotter than the others. When it stops, everything that is melted off during the first incursion comes back but is again burned off and the pain is much greater than the previous time. These reoccurring fire pits are like teasing through a temporary relief.

Psalms 140:10 (ESV)
"Let burning coals fall upon them! Let them be cast into fire, into miry pits, no more to rise!"

A sin on earth is a hundred times worse in Hell. The pain is amplified in immeasurable ways. The worst part about the sin, no matter how great or small, is that in Hell the sin is transformed into a perversion of what it was!

It was revealed to me that a sin can lead you straight to Hell if not forgiven for it. So, that means you must be clean if you want to pass through those pearly gates, and you must know someone just to get into heaven like the Son of the Living God! As I went deeper into hell, I saw these cells with people in them. Then one of the demons came with a spear in hand, went over to one of the cell doors, opened it and stabbed a host of these unfortunate souls; like a human shish kabob. The cell door shut as the demon walked off in the distance filled with laughter, and all these poor souls draped over its shoulder cried in sheer horror!

I was in total conflict of my senses. As I looked elsewhere, I noticed there were a lot of demons congregating in one area which had a giant bon fire raging on. As these nasty things gathered around the bon fire, something ghastly came out of it. It was that thing that looked like Shrek! Some of the demons cheered while others flung curses. Now I've heard curse words before, but to hear a curse word in hell would cut deep into your very soul. The mere sound and meaning were seriously amplified! This Shrek thing had some announcements, but I didn't really pay attention, so I just wandered around some more. I came upon some old ruins with something familiar about them. It appears Satan tried to recreate Heaven. Satan tries to imitate any and everything that comes from the Father God!

As I went through these ruins, I came to a building that had demons going into it, almost like a gathering of some sort, so I followed. I stumbled right in the middle of a meeting filled with the most horrid looking creatures all discussing how they could be able to fill different lives with misery, afflictions in lust and constant turmoil. Suddenly, Satan violently burst through one of the demons and the room was filled with laughter, but I didn't see anything funny about it! These demons couldn't see or hear me, as a matter of fact, they could pass right through me, but I wasn't about to put it to the test. At times, these demons would look right into my direction as if they were looking at me.

Satan greeted all these demons by flinging curses at them as they flung them back at him with me in the crossfire. I felt so filthy while words were being exchanged and apparently it was funny. As Satan walked to the center of the room, there was a vulture on his shoulder that would vomit on his back and face every few minutes. Satan spoke on how he had just received permission from God for the temptation of certain people. When this was said, all the demons cheered with glee. The celebration was cut short because Satan also added that there were rules to be followed.

Job 1:8-12 (ESV)

And the LORD said to Satan, "Have you considered my servant Job, that there is none like him on the earth, a blameless and upright man, who fears God and turns away from evil?" Then Satan answered the LORD and said, "Does Job fear God for no reason? Have you not put a hedge around him and his house and all that he has, on every side?

You have blessed the work of his hands, and his possessions have increased in the land. But stretch out your hand and touch all that he has, and he will curse you to your face." And the LORD said to Satan, "Behold, all that he has is in your hand. Only against him do not stretch out your hand." So, Satan went out from the presence of the LORD.

My memory was jogged to the fact that the vision I had some time before was that of when I was in the heavenly court! Every one of those demons expressed how they wanted to make so many people pay for becoming Born Again Christians. But even as devious as they all are, these demons still had to obey Gods Law and not go beyond any boundaries that were set before them. Despite how any of the demons felt, they all had no choice in the matter but to respect Gods Law! The name of the Father is so powerful, and the blood of Christ is untouchable. Even though, every demon hates anything that has to do with God the Father or Jesus Christ the Son, the respect that Satan and his fallen angels give was simply amazing! As I stood there listening to everything that was being discussed, one of the demons spoke out about the Mark (666) and if it could be set in place.

The ones who willingly take the Mark of the Beast (666), their Souls are lost to Satan without any redemption!

Revelations 13:11-18, 14:9-11 (ESV)

"Then I saw another beast rising out of the earth. It had two horns like a lamb, and it spoke like a dragon.

It exercises all the authority of the first beast in its presence and makes the earth and its inhabitants worship the first beast, whose mortal wound was healed.

It performs great signs, even making fire come down from heaven to earth in front of people, and by the signs that it is allowed to work in the presence of the beast it deceives those who dwell on earth, telling them to make an image for the beast that was wounded by the sword and yet lived.

And it was allowed to give breath to the image of the beast, so that the image of the beast might even speak and might cause those who would not worship the image of the beast to be slain.

Also, it causes all, both small and great, both rich and poor, both free and slave, to be marked on the right hand or the forehead, so that no one can buy or sell unless he has the mark, that is, the name of the beast or the number of its name. This calls for wisdom: let the one who has understanding calculate the number of the beast, for it is the number of a man, and his number is 666."

"And another angel, a third, followed them, saying with a loud voice, "If anyone worships the beast and its image and receives a mark on his forehead or on his hand, he also will drink the wine of God's wrath, poured full strength into the cup of his anger, and he will be tormented with fire and sulfur in the presence of the holy angels and in the presence of the Lamb. And the smoke of their torment goes up forever and ever, and they have no rest, day or night, these worshipers of the beast and its image, and whoever receives the mark of its name."

With much grief in his voice, Satan cried, "No," and then he added "Because God said it wasn't time, so until then, tell me of the good news you each have for me."

The Shrek thing stood up and explained how they have successfully filled as many people as they could with lust, gossip, pride, prejudice in many forms and some a religious sprit with most of these afflictions finding homes inside regular church goers. Then he added how tough it is that more churches are being Holy Ghost filled every day! The next topic on their agenda was to fill as many hearts and minds with so much fear that it would be near impossible to save anyone. **But through Gods saving grace, all things are possible!**

Satan then asked about the witchcraft project. One of the demons stood up and proclaimed that, "If we are to attack people's minds so that they would be vulnerable as an open door, then I'm going to need more demons to help me. Too many people are being saved and at an early age too!" Satan added that they all needed to twist whatever thoughts each person has then to also work on the confusion, because it helps make chaos that much easier. "And we need to work on getting homosexuality in as many churches and lives as we can. But when you're doing this, make sure to first push in compromise, and don't forget about hate, slip that in too!" I left their meeting as they were talking about Reality Television shows and wondered over to another building where it was quiet, then I kneeled to pray.

After some time, I stood to my feet, looked around and then I heard a faint sound coming from outside the room that I was in. I followed the sound to this enormous pit that was pitch black. I backed up, turned around and without as much as a sound uttered from my lips, I walked away! Walking through the streets of Hell, I noticed the strange twisted view of this place and how it's supposed to resemble Heaven but only as an imitation. Not to mention that Satan does have a good memory of what Heaven looked like before he was cast out. Lucifer was indeed an angel that resided over Gods' throne and controlled the music. Instead of being humble, he wanted it all for himself, so he brain-washed a third of the angels to follow him. Lucifer acted as though he was supposed to be God. He was then cast out of Heaven for starting a war!

Luke 10:18 (ESV)

And he said to them, "I saw Satan fall like lightning from heaven."

It is true that Lucifer was cast out of Heaven by the Word of God. Even though this action wasn't completed physically by Him but by one of His Mighty Angels,' that's one example of just how powerful God is. He didn't even have to lift a finger or spend time on a thought and Lucifer was gone! Lucifer fell from Heaven like a bolt of lightning and hit the earth with that of an impact or the likeness of a massive meteor. Now Lucifer is a Devil with a title which is called 'Satan.' Everything Satan can't touch he copies and tries to pawn it off as the original.

Revelation 12:7-12 (ESV)

"Now war arose in heaven, Michael and his angels fighting against the dragon. And the dragon and his angels fought back, but he was defeated, and there was no longer any place for them in heaven. And the great dragon was thrown down, that ancient serpent, who is called the devil and Satan, the deceiver of the whole world-he was thrown down to the earth, and his angels were thrown down with him.

And I heard a loud voice in heaven, saying, "Now the salvation and the power and the kingdom of our God and the authority of his Christ have come, for the accuser of our brothers has been thrown down, who accuses them day and night before our God.

And they have conquered him by the blood of the Lamb and by the word of their testimony, for they loved not their lives even unto death. Therefore, rejoice, O heavens and you who dwell in them! But woe to you, O earth and sea, for the devil has come down to you in great wrath, because he knows that his time is short!"

I was relieved that I wasn't going to spend the rest of my life in Hell, then suddenly, I came across an escapee. In my path was a tortured soul hiding as if something was hunting him. This thought just came to me, 'How did he escape?'

His past became so clear to me as if he himself were telling me of his past deeds. He let an addiction send him to Hell when all he had to do was ask God the Father to forgive him of his sins, then give him the strength and the will power to be sincere in his heart. So, whenever that addiction pops its ugly head, he'd have all the strength he'll need against the devil! His reasoning, whatever it was just wasn't enough to keep him from here.

If you need the Lord's help, just ask and He'll help you through any trial, but you must want to be helped. Don't tie the Fathers hands if He's the only one who can help you! Be diligent in your ways and trust in the Lord always. Be truthful to yourself and be sincere to God, because God knows your own heart better than you! I wish he would've realized that before this area became his destination!

A Sin has no size comparison, a Sin has no precedence over another Sin, a Sin isn't worse than another Sin; all Sins are equal to each other and can equally send you to Hell! A lie is the same as Bestiality, these are both Sins and these are both the same.

1 John 3:1-10   (ESV)

"See what kind of love the Father has given to us, that we should be called children of God; and so, we are. The reason why the world does not know us is that it did not know him. Beloved, we are God's children now, and what we will be has not yet appeared; but we know that when he appears, we shall be like him, because we shall see him as he is. And everyone who thus hopes in him purifies himself as he is pure. Everyone who makes a practice of sinning also practices lawlessness; sin is lawlessness.

You know that he appeared to take away sins, and in him there is no sin. No one who abides in him keeps on sinning; no one who keeps on sinning has either seen him or known him. Little children, let no one deceive you. Whoever practices righteousness is righteous, as he is righteous.

Whoever makes a practice of sinning is of the devil, for the devil has been sinning from the beginning. The reason the Son of God appeared was to destroy the works of the devil. No one born of God makes a practice of sinning, for God's seed abides in him, and he cannot keep on sinning because he has been born of God.

By this it is evident who are the children of God, and who are the children of the devil: whoever does not practice righteousness is not of God, nor is the one who does not love his brother."

As I walked away, I heard a painful scream followed by a slashing sound and a demonic sounding voice filled with laughter that cried, "Tag...Your it!" At this point, I kept on walking with out as much as a look. Then this thought came to me, a somewhat condescending thought, 'Well, I guess his addiction found him!' The more I walked, the more disgusted, frustrated and disorientated I felt, so I moved on with slight confusion. As I walked on, it turned into a run then I wanted to get away. So, I jumped as hard as I could and hoped it would turn into flight, but I fell hard, face first into the ground. I crossed my breaking point with the feeling of defeat, and I found myself on my knees crying then praying because the peace that I'd felt before was not there anymore.

I felt stronger as the words came from my Redeemer to my head, **"Peace be Still and stay strong my son for your journey is a just one!"** I said out loud, "Not Funny Jesus, get me out of here! Then immediately I thought to myself, 'Maybe I shouldn't be so unruly to the Lord.'

Psalms 83:1 (ESV)

"O God, do not keep silence; do not hold your peace or be still, O God!"

Isaiah 42:14 (ESV)

"For a long time, I have held my peace; I have kept still and restrained myself; now I will cry out like a woman in labor; I will gasp and pant."

I felt the presence of the Lord lift from me and then I was truly alone. I started walking but this time it was very different as fear gripped my heart like something terrible. I urinated on myself and it got worse. I couldn't control my own actions or bodily functions! The black air is so thick, you can't breathe or sleep in Hell. It was as though I was being smothered and remembering this horrible thickness. I had trouble seeing, but I could see barely enough to know that I didn't want to be there anymore. I felt so filthy and my clothing withered away. My skin felt like it was rotting away. What was left of my skin spontaneously combusted into flames causing me the most unbearable pain!

The ground under my feet turned smooth with a slimy feel to it. It was almost like walking on rather large rubber hoses with something slippery covered on them, but these things seem to be moving in different directions. With a lump in my throat followed by the beating of my heart through my chest, I reached down to feel just what I was standing on. Suddenly but slowly, the mist that was around my feet cleared and to my surprise I was standing on snakes! These snakes were biting me as I ran to safety, wherever that was. Something big grabbed me, but I broke free and continued to run as fast as I could. I really couldn't see all that well, but I knew to run away from the laughter!

My run was cut short as I ran into something big and hairy. Whatever it was, bit me hard across my neck and back then with the sound of flesh ripping and feeling its teeth drag across my body as I was tossed into one of the fire pits. I was simply Horrified with terror as I tried to claw my way to the top, but the pit grew deeper the closer I came to the top. Then I heard wings coming in my direction. Whatever it was had sharp claws because it dug deep into my shoulders. It lifted me up from the pit and flung me through the black air. As I flew uncontrollably through the air with a relentless force, I was instantly struck in the back by something so powerful that I cried out in anguish. The impact caused me to fly forward like a leaf helplessly moving in the wind.

Then I was struck again and again, insanely enough it did remind me of a tennis match, but with every blow that I suffered just sent me spinning and flipping through the air to my next designation. This painful torture went on for more than I would like to remember! Then in midflight, I felt excruciating pain shoot up and down my leg and through my back as a clawed hand grabbed my leg. This monsters' claws dug through my skin pulling me down and slamming me hard to the ground. Then it flung me through the air ripping me as it let go of my leg.

As soon as I hit the ground, another demon grabbed my other leg and dragged me through sharp rocks as my skin and wounds were being ripped open followed by the snakes as they bit me over and over with no mercy! The demon threw me several feet in the air, and when I came falling, I hit the ground so hard I heard bones cracking. Then I waited for something else to happen, but for a few minutes nothing did, so I took off. By this time, my soul had dimmed to a dirty gray. I was in disbelief as I cried out to God for help, but the realization of me being on my own had set in. Then I started to feel curses wanting to come out but feeling desolate I asked for forgiveness while I ran! Then I stopped and tried to clean myself off, but it didn't do any good at all.

Suddenly I heard the thunderous sound of wings heading into my direction again. Whatever it was, bit me hard on my back drawing more blood out. I felt my life draining out and away from me! There I was running through Hell covered in my own waste and blood. I ran a great distance with my sorrows on display but feeling weak and rundown. There was absolutely no safety anywhere. Then out from nowhere, this vulture appeared then started to slash me. My strength was just about gone from trying to fight this bird off, and then with no warning, this grotesque creature vomited on my face, neck and back causing a great temperamental strength to come upon me.

Self-acting but unintentional, my wounds healed and caused me great relief, but only for a moment. Then spontaneously, my wounds reopened deeper and I felt weaker than before. The vultures' vomit healed my wounds and gave me strength temporally, but it made me feel even worse than before causing me greater pain. This went on for some time, and then in a spilt second... I was staring up into the sky with the feeling of being safe. "What a relief, I'm not in Hell anymore!" That's just what I thought when the scenery had changed. How did it change?

Souls at Night

An Abrasion for some while others still Fight,

A Candidate of Aggression through this Near Sight;

A Peace from Depression taken by Flight,

A Whelm of Pressure through a show of Might;

To Weakness from Kindness mistaken in Spite,

From Hate to Love in feelings Contrite;

In Blissful movement for Wronging a Right,

Through Deep Emotions to cater Polite;

Statement through Meaning carefree as a kite,

Through Pain a Healing to Day from Night;

Help from above it's not our Fight,

His Love rains down like a Meteorite;

My Pain no more through Wisdom His site,

Our chaos to folly from Darkness to Light;

Not our Battle for sure our Lord will Smite,

A means to an End a Beginning in sight;

Evil no shame through Jesus our Might,

For God's Protection our Souls at Night!

To Be Continued...

www.ingramcontent.com/pod-product-compliance
Lightning Source LLC
Chambersburg PA
CBHW080454170426
43196CB00016B/2800